PUB WALKS
IN DORSET

Forty Circular Walks

BRACE OF
PHEASANTS

Around Dorset Inns

Mike Power

"As a service to civilisation this book ranks alongside the wheel and the automatic cash dispenser" - Alan Jones. Blackmore Vale Magazine. April 89.

"A book which must be added to every serious Dorset walkers - and serious Dorset drinker's shelf of reference books"
- Rufus Castle. Dorset County Magazine. June 89.

Other Publications in the series.
"40 More Pub Walks in Dorset".
"Pub Walks in Hampshire and the I.O.W."
"Pub Walks in Devon".
"Pub Walks in Cornwall".
"Pub Walks in West Sussex".
"Pub Walks in East Sussex".
"Pub Walks in Kent".
"Pub Walks in The New Forest".

30,000 copies already sold
1st edition - published March 1989
2nd edition - published August 1989
3rd edition - published February 1990
4th edition - published February 1991
5th edition - published December 1993
6th edition - published March 1997 (completely revised)

Acknowledgements
I would like to thank my wife Cicely for supporting me, sometimes up to her knees in mud on many of the exploratory walks, to the many tenants and landlords for their cooperation and Eddie Hams for his much appreciated assistance.

ISBN 0-9514502-0-4

Publisher's note
Whilst every care has been taken to ensure the accuracy of all the information given in this book errors will occur due to many factors. Paths can be re-routed, stiles can replace gates and pubs frequently change hands. Neither the printers nor the publishers can accept responsibility for any inaccuracies.

Power Publications
1, Clayford Ave, Ferndown
Dorset. BH22 9PQ.

Printed by Pardy & Son (Printers) Ltd, Ringwood, Hants.

Front cover: The Brace of Pheasants, Plush

INTRODUCTION

When I put this collection of walks together in 1988 the majority of paths were unsigned and in poor condition even close scrutiny of the definitive maps did not help so I undertook my own research on the ground and spoke to the landowners where possible - you did the rest. Today I am happy to see the majority are well marked and walked on a regular basis. This updated edition includes changes that have taken place with the addition of some new paths plus a new report for each pub.

All the pubs included in this book have been chosen either for their charm or their proximity to a lovely walk, no charge whatsoever is made for inclusion in this book. The walks are planned to start at the pub on the assumption that you wish to partake of their hospitality, on the rare occasion you do not we respectfully ask you to refrain from using their car park; where practicable we have listed alternative areas but of course there is no reason why you should not park at a convenient point anywhere along the route.

It is the legal duty of all landowners to maintain the upkeep of public paths and rights of way across their property. Always remember it is an offence to obstruct a public footpath. You have the right to remove as much of the obstruction as necessary to allow free passage, but not to cause wilful damage to property. If the obstruction cannot be removed you have the right to leave the path and walk round the obstruction causing no more damage than is necessary, in the case of crops the path must be trodden afresh even if it means treading on them.

On the 13th August 1990 a new "Rights of Way" act became law, primarily to deal with the problem of ploughed and blocked paths. Under the new law the farmer must make good the surface within 24 hours of the disturbance (two weeks) if the disturbance is the first one for a particular crop. It must have a minimum width of one metre and two metres for a bridlepath, and the exact line of the path must be apparent on the ground. You should report any problems you find to the Rights of Way Officer at Dorset County Council, Dorchester.

Walking is extremely good for you and the best way to explore the countryside but a few simple rules must be observed. Take care in the absence of pavements keeping where possible to the right-hand side of the road, wear suitable clothing - quick drying, light weight trousers are best even in summer as many paths become overgrown with nettles. Footwear should be well treaded and waterproof. A walking stick is an ideal accompaniment for clearing the path and testing the stability of the ground ahead. Other handy items are a compass, and if walking late in the evening a torch. I also advise people to carry the relevant Ordnance Survey map. The references in the book refer to the 1:5000,000 – $1\frac{1}{4}$ inch to the mile – Landranger series. Those covering Dorset are Nos. 183, 184, 193, 194 and 195.

Wherever you go always respect the country code. Guard against all fires, fasten gates, keep dogs under control and always on a lead where livestock are present, keep to the path across farm land, take all litter home, respect wildlife and do not dig up or pick wild flowers and plants.

I regularly enjoy all these walks and the hospitality of the pubs. I hope you will too.

Mike Power 1997.

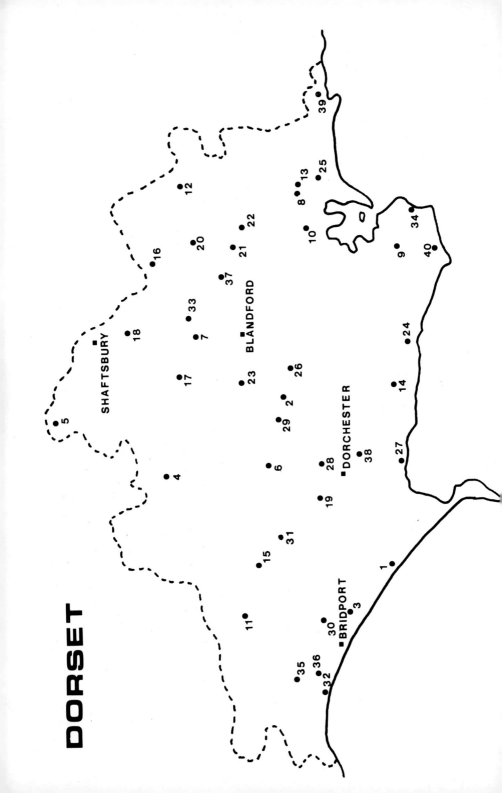

DORSET

SHAFTSBURY

BLANDFORD

DORCHESTER

BRIDPORT

CONTENTS

The Ilchester Arms, Abbotsbury

The Ilchester Arms is an interesting old inn dating from the late 16th-century. It was once an old coaching stop known then as The Ship having just the one beamed bar and has been associated on the past both with royalty and smuggling. The inn has been added to over the years and now comprises several linked rooms, all with heavily beamed ceilings and part panelled walls adorned with a wealth of old pictures, copper, brass and miscellanea including a large stuffed fish in a case above the inglenook fireplace where a warm log fire burns on cold winter days. A mix of comfortable chairs and assorted tables complete the atmosphere. At the back is a sunny conservatory and a small lawned area with picnic benches.

Three real ales served by hand pump in this Greenalls pub are Flowers Original, Wadworth 6X and Draught Bass.

An extensive bar menu is served seven days a week which apart from snacks like homemade soup, various ploughman's and salads, daily specials might include slithers of home-baked ham with Cumberland sauce or baked Florida avocado with prawns and a cheese sauce. There is a daily roast, various steaks, pies and usually a freshly cooked curry. Other dishes often listed are braised Dorset lamb in a rich red wine and rosemary sauce and tender pieces of Cumbrian pork cooked in a casserole with paprika, caraway and finished with cream. African stew is a full hearted secret dish with pineapple and peppers in a rich sauce.

The inn is open all day during the week from 11 a.m. till 11 p.m.

Children are welcome in the areas away from the bar but no dogs.

The inn has ten letting rooms the majority of which have en-suite bathrooms/showers.

Telephone: (01305) 871243.

Pub situated in the centre of the village on the B3157.

Approx. distance of walk: 3 miles OS Map 194 SY 575/854.

Car park at the rear of the pub through the arch also ample street parking and free car park close by.

Abbotsbury is a typical pretty Dorset village situated in a sheltered valley close to the well known Chesil Beach. Hilly but compensated by stunning scenery the walk takes you first past the famous sub-tropical gardens then along the Dorset Coast Path towards the Swannery and finally to St Catherines Chapel, high on the hill.

Turn left from the inn walking the short distance up West Street until you reach Chapel Lane on the left. Follow the track turning right upon reaching the barn then left at the next track which leads to a farm gate. Pass through onto the bridleway and turn right walking up to meet the road.

Turn left then fork left on the road signposted, to Chesil Beach. Your route takes you past the sub-tropical Gardens at Abbotsbury well worth a visit if you have the time. The gardens are open all year round from 10 a.m. till 5 p.m. (3 p.m. in the winter). At the bottom of the hill turn left into the car park, walk across to the bridge on the right and turn left along Chesil Beach. Follow the coastal path beside the hedge then pass through the gate onto the track beside the Fleet Sanctuary.

Continue walking away from the shore until you reach a stile on the right signposted, to the Swannery. Enter the field walking up and across to the gate on the far side close to a wartime fortification. Maintain direction around the hillside where you will find a path marker stone. Turning right will take you down to the world famous Swannery, open 7 days a week from early March to the end of October. If you are not in to hill climbing the road leads back to the village otherwise make the steep climb to the chapel at the top. Built by the Benedictine Monks between 1376 and 1401 it has served as a landmark to sailors over the centuries.

Leave the chapel and head down in the direction of the village, through a series of gates then along the track and, just before reaching the road look for a small path on the right which leads directly into the car park at the back of the pub.

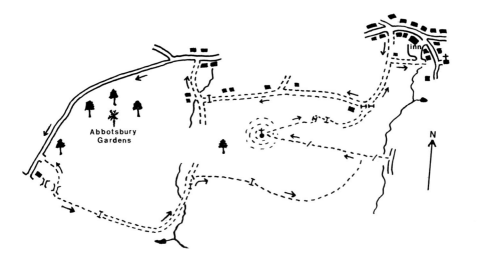

Abbotsbury
Gardens

inn

N

The Fox Inn, Ansty

The Fox is a charming flint and brick built inn in the heart of Dorset. It was originally the home of the Woodhouse family who later joined with local brewer, Charles Hall to form the Blandford brewery. The inn has been privately owned for a number of years but was bought back by the brewery in 1996. All credit to Hall & Woodhouse for the excellent refurbishment job restoring the house to its former glory. Leading from the flagstone porch and hall are two very attractive and comfortable bars, one displaying a large collection of old family photographs. There is a beautiful, three quarter wood panelled dining room with an interesting mix of furnishings, a family room and skittle alley.

Badger Best and Tanglefoot are just two of Hall & Woodhouses' range of real ales on offer.

The Fox has always been renowned for its food; in 1980 Egon Ronay chose the inn as his first 'Pub of the Year'. Served all week the imaginative menu lists several ploughman's - one with lobster and avocado, baked potatoes and freshly baked rustic bread sandwiches, also snacks which include grilled venison sausages with bubble & squeak and honey glazed ham and eggs. A choice of starters on the menu include homemade soup, duck liver pate and deep fried tortelloni with blue cheese dressing followed by supreme of chicken, bacon and Stilton en croute served with a Port and Stilton sauce, grilled fillet of salmon 'a la meuniere' Griskin of pork 'Normande' with caramelized apple and brandy sauce and homemade leek and Roquefort tart all served with jacket or saute potatoes.

Weekday opening times are from 11 a.m till 3 p.m. and 7 p.m. till 11 p.m.

Families and dogs equally welcome.

Overnight accommodation available.

Telephone: (01258) 880328.

Village can be reached from several directions the most direct from the A354 Blandford to Puddletown road. Take the Milton Abbas turning at Milbourne St Andrews then go left at the junction of Hewish Farm following the signs for Ansty.

Approx. distance of walk: 3½ miles. OS Map 194 ST 765/033.

There is ample parking at the front and around the inn.

A very pleasant scenic and hilly walk mostly across farm land and along peaceful country lanes taking in the famed Dorset Gap. As it can often be very muddy in the winter the best time is late spring especially as the primroses and other wild flowers are at their best.

Leave the inn turning left and in a few paces look for the footpath on the right beside 'Brewery Cottage'. Walk up to the stile, enter the field and bear right down to the metal gate, cross the brook and head up the field making for the stile in the top right-hand corner turning right into the farm road.

Follow this metalled lane up past Cothayes Farm to Melcombe Park Farm bearing right then left up through the farmyard and out through the gate at the back. Ahead of you are two similar gates, pass through the one on the right and, keeping fairly close to woods on the right arc right up the hillside making for a small metal gate set in the far hedge.

Bear left along the ridge and after meeting the sunken track follow it down to the gate and into the Dorset Gap. A book is kept in a green tin on the right if you wish to record your visit. Quite a collection have built up over the years which make interesting reading. I have walked here at various times of the year but undoubtedly the prettiest is in late spring when the surrounding hills are carpeted with primroses.

Leave the Gap and take the sunken path immediately on the left down between the hills, through the farm gate and into a field. Keep straight ahead beside the hedge, through two more gates maintaining direction to one last gate then turn left onto the tarred farm road. Walk up to the crossroads at Melcombe Bingham and turn left back to the pub. As there are no pavements at first keep to the right-hand side until you reach the small attractive village.

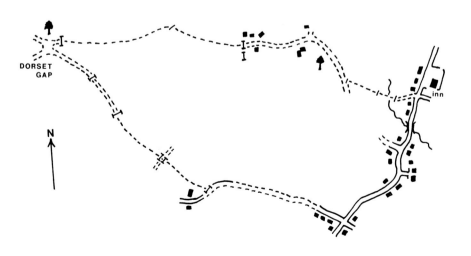

The Spyway Inn, Askerswell

The small village of Askerwesll, lying in the shadow of Eggardon Hill, is barely half a mile from the busy A35 yet remains one of the most peaceful and unspoilt areas of Dorset.

Positioned above the village The Spyway's enviable position affords glorious views of the surrounding hills. Festooned with flowers in summer, this friendly local inn has two bars, the largest of which has a solid brick fireplace with wood burning stove, light coloured furniture and a large collection of cups displayed on the ceiling beams. A grandfather clock, high back wooden settles and a herring bone brickwork bar characterize the smaller room. The separate attractive dining room has part brick walls and pine country furniture on a quarry tiled floor. Outside there is a beautifully kept garden and beer terrace.

The inn is a freehouse well run by the resident owners, Don and Jackie Roderick. Three real ales regularly available are Ruddles County, Adnams Southwold Bitter and Ushers Best. The wine list is good with 24 bins all uniquely priced in 1996 at £6-95 which no doubt contributed to the winning of the 'Carlsberg Tetley Pub Wine List Winner of the Year' award.

A wide choice of very good home cooked food is served daily and includes assorted ploughman's, Spyway sausage and chips, seafood platter, omelettes and steaks. Daily specials might include butterfly prawns, individual homemade lasagne, half a roast chicken, chilli and homemade seafood pasta, plus vegetarian meals such as homemade leek and Stilton quiche and homemade mushroom, leek and courgette bake. Sweets range from baked bananas in brandy to homemade chocolate and brandy mousse.

Weekday opening times are from 11 a.m. till 2.30 p.m. and 6 p.m. till 11 p.m.

No children under 14 or dogs allowed in any of the bars.

Telephone: (01308) 485250.

Askerswell is signed from the A35 between Dorchester and Bridport. Enter the village, turn right and then immediately left up the hill turning left at the junction.

Approx. distance of walk: 4½ miles OS Map 194 SY 528/934.

There are parking areas either side of the inn with space for a couple of cars in the lane at the front.

One of my favourite scenic walks in this lovely peaceful and attractive area of Dorset, at first through this pretty award winning village and then along farm tracks and field paths high up onto Haydon Down. It is fairly hilly, a little demanding and apart from the occasional muddy patch good underfoot.

From the pub turn right up the hill and right again back down the lane to the village. Turn left at the crossroads and progress up the hill as far as minor crossroads turning left. Walk only as far as the first dwelling on the right where, to the left of the entrance is a wide farm gate. Pass through into the field and bear left up to the gate close to a row of conifers. Enter the field turning left and, keeping close to the boundary walk to the crossing point on the far side, climb over onto the concrete farm road and turn right. Follow this undulating drive, through a metal gate and further on pass through the small gate left of the cattle grid into Nallers Farm. Cross the brook, walk up to the farm house and immediately turn right though the metal gate. Keep to the grass track ahead, through a similar gate walking beside the wire fence eventually reaching a stile beside a gate. Climb into the field and arc left round the hillside making for the stable block on the far side. Pass through

the gate (muddy at times) and turn left through a second gate climbing the well trodden path up the hillside to the gate.

Follow the limestone track ahead which rises steeply uphill, under the power lines and into a field. Keep straight ahead until you reach an enclosed field on the left, pass through the metal gate and maintain direction up towards the barn. At the top turn left onto the grass track walking down through a couple of gates and into the lane.

Stride across into the field opposite and bear left down the hillside, right of the electricity pole where you will find a sunken grass track leading gently downhill then beside a hedge to a small wooden gate at the bottom. Turn right down the grass track then left along the track to the gate, out onto the drive and turn left. Pass through a second gate and continue down the tarred drive enjoying the glorious scenery before reaching the lane then turn right back to the pub.

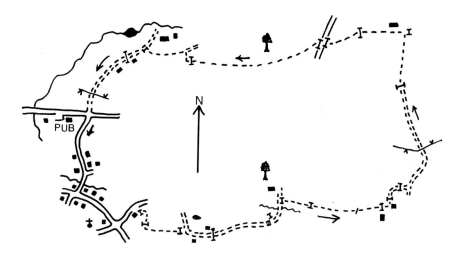

The White Hart, Bishops Caundle

The White Hart is a two story brick-built inn dating from the 16th-century, the front being added two centuries later. It was once a coaching stop, a horse mounting block can still be seen at the front. Handsome ancient beams, low bowed ceilings, bare stone walls, wood panelling and an open fireplace are attractive features of the irregularly-shaped main bar. There is a separate dining area, a skittle alley which doubles as a function room and a beer garden with excellent childrens' play area.

Owned by Hall & Woodhouse and very well run by the present licensees the pub is popular with locals and various groups who use it regularly as a meeting place. There are two real ales, Badger Best and Tanglefoot.

Good mostly home-cooked bar food, available from 12 noon till 2.30 p.m. and 7 p.m till 9.30 p.m, offers the usual snacks like ploughman's and sandwiches plus interesting daily specials which might include faggots; chicken and Stilton roulade - breast of chicken filled with Stilton butter, wrapped in bacon and cooked in red wine, navarine of lamb, pork in orange and ginger and chicken Alexander - chicken breast in a creamy brandy and mustard sauce. From the extensive set menu there is a good selection of starters such as coronation chicken, homemade chicken liver and brandy pate and crispy coated broccoli followed by various grills and fish dishes including a tasty fish pie, also old English steak, stir fried chicken in a black bean sauce, apricot glazed chicken, speciality pies and Somerset cider bake - diced gammon and leeks in a cider cheese sauce topped with Cheddar. Vegetarians have a choice of meals like Brie and broccoli bake and there is a good choice for children. Included on the large sweet list are homemade sponge puddings.

Opening times are from 11 a.m. till 2.30 p.m. and 6.30 p.m till 11 p.m.

Overnight accommodation is available.

Telephone: (01963) 23301

Bishops Caundle is on the A3030 running between the A357, Blandford to Sturminster Newton road and the A352 Dorchester to Sherborne road.

Approx. distance of walk: 4¾ miles. OS Map 194 ST 696/133.

There is a good sized car park at the side of the inn plus two lay-bys in the main road at the front.

An enjoyable, peaceful walk in the beautiful Blackmoor Vale, at first across farm land towards Holtwood before reaching an attractive woodland bridleway, thereafter on field paths and peaceful country lanes. Although not too demanding some areas can be extremely muddy in the winter.

From the pub cross the road, turn right and go through the gate into the small field on the left, signposted. Walk to the gate opposite and head across to a couple of stiles and track, over a stile in the wire fence maintaining direction towards two more stiles and plank bridge. Enter the field and turn immediately left heading for the stile in the far hedge (left of the oak tree). Keep to the hedgerow then enter the field on the right. Staying close to the hedge walk almost to the end of the field, pass through the gap into the adjoining field and turn left. Cross to the stile in the hedge, enter the field making for the farm gate opposite and turn left into the lane.

Keep walking for some distance until you reach the crossroads then go straight across into the lane opposite. It descends gently down between attractive young woodland. At the bend turn left and join the footpath signposted, to Holt Lane. The path shares the bridleway for a short distance. After passing over a very pretty gully turn right ignoring the gate ahead. This very attractive bridleway descends gradually downhill with fields on the left and a pretty brook and woods on the right, although usually good underfoot it can become muddy in places during the winter.

On the left at the bottom is a gate (opposite a stile), pass through into the field here and bear left across to the small wooden gate, climb the crossing point into the field and turn right. Walk up towards the farm buildings and near the top pass through the gate into the field on the right, turning left past the silage pit and make for the gate at the right-hand side of the barn. Walk to the gate ahead then to the left of the barn, up the track then right, through the gate and up to the road.

Carefully cross over to the metal gate opposite and bear right down to the gate in the far corner of the field. Keep straight ahead beside the hedge then enter the thicket on the left following the beaten path up to the farm gate, into the field bearing right down to the gate located to the left of the thatched cottage turning left into the lane.

Cross the road, keep straight ahead at the crossroads, walk for a while and take the next lane on the left. Continue ahead over a minor crossroads turning left when eventually reaching the junction. Walk up the hill and turn right into Brown Street. After rounding a couple of bends ignore the first stile on the left but continue ahead until you come to the field entrance beside another stile then bear right following the well trodden path across the field to the gate in the far hedge finally turning left back to the pub.

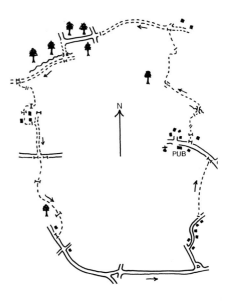

The White Lion, Bourton

The White Lion, built in 1723 and known locally as "The Bush", is the most northerly inn in Dorset close to both the Somerset and Wiltshire borders. It is an attractive, warm and friendly inn partially covered with climbing roses. From the moment you enter through the low front door, glimpse the small cosy bars, smell the aroma of wood smoke and walk on original flagstone floors you know immediately you are in a genuine Dorset pub. A small flight of steps lead to a separate fifty-five cover dining room and there is a large fully enclosed beer garden.

The leasehold of this pub is now owned by three partners, Helen and Mike Rogerson and Madeleine Styler all of whom live on the premises and work in the business full time. Real ales include Ushers Best, Directors Bitter and Old Speckled Hen.

The inn has always been popular for its excellent food and has just recently received praise both from Egon Ronay and The Good Food Guide. Employing two chefs the majority of dishes, home-cooked and freshly prepared on the premises range from bar snacks such as ploughman's, tasty homemade soup, sandwiches and jacket potatoes to a full a la carte menu. Constantly changing the list might include Barbary duck served pink with a blackcurrant sauce, medallions of pork tenderloin on a bed of noodles with orange and ginger sauce, supreme of perch, lightly grilled monkfish tails served with a compote of Mediterranean tomatoes and a fillet of pink bream with a Champagne sauce. Also curries, pasta, vegetarian dishes, an extended fish menu, sumptuous sweets, a separate childrens' menu and a Sunday roast.

Dogs and families are made really welcome.

Superb en-suite accommodation is available.

Weekday opening times are from 11.45 a.m. till 3 p.m. and 6 p.m. till 11 p.m. Telephone: (01747) 840866.

The inn is in High Street, opposite the junction where the B3092 meets the old A303.

Approx. distance of walk: 4½ miles OS Map 183 ST 778/308.

Park in the road at the front, in the small parking area opposite or the car park at the side of the pub.

An extremely enjoyable country walk in this the most northerly tip of Dorset. It could aptly be called "The Three Counties Walk", because although it begins in Dorset it actually passes through both Wiltshire and Somerset. The walk, hilly in places, takes you across farm land, through woods, over streams and along established paths and peaceful country lanes. Although fairly easy going it can sometimes be muddy underfoot.

Turn left from the inn and a short distance up the lane pass through the kissing gate into the field on the left. Bearing slightly left follow the well trodden path to a similar gate in the far corner, go through onto the wide grass track following it down and round between fields to the right, then through the small gate on the left and out through the farm gate into the lane.

Cross over, past a couple of cottages and just before the entrance to Bullpits Farm pass through the small gate into the field on the right turning left. Cross the golf course to the gate in the far corner, go out into the lane and turn left. It is here that the three counties meet; the spot is marked by Ecgberht's Stone which can be seen, mounted on a small plinth, on the opposite side of the river that runs through the golf course.

Follow the road downhill into Pen Selwood, or Penselwood as it is shown on the map, over the bridge, and just past a cluster of cottages take the signed footpath on the right between a barn and double garage signposted, Coombe Street & Pear Ash. Join this narrow path up to the gate, across the yard and through the kissing gate into the field opposite following the well beaten path up the hillside gradually bearing left across

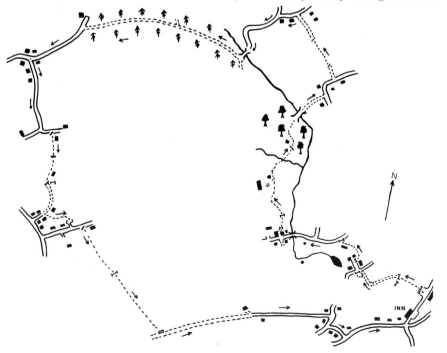

to the right-hand side of a row of cottages where a stile allows access to a narrow path. Almost immediately cross the stile into the field on the right, walk down to the brook carefully crossing to the far side and walk up the bank to the stile in the hedge by the thatched cottage. Follow this very attractive, undulating path through the wood and down to a bridge then up the fenced path turning left into the lane at the top.

Walk for a short distance, and as you round the right-hand bend turn left onto the narrow grass track. Ignore the stile on the right but pass through the gate into the field keeping straight ahead to the stile opposite then along the attractive narrow path turning left into the lane.

Walk down past a couple of cottages then fork left down the hill crossing the bridge at the bottom and take the track on the right, just before reaching the white entrance gates to Swallowfield. This wide, sometimes muddy but very attractive track, rises steadily through bluebell woods. At the top turn

left following this quiet lane into Pear Ash then left again in the centre.

Reasonably straight at first the road then bears right at which point turn left towards the farm, and almost immediately cross the stile into the field on the right. Walk to the stile in the fence opposite, maintaining direction to the stiles in the far hedge and head across the field to the stile beside the gate. Go over onto the path, enter the cul-de-sac then immediately turn left and join the tarred path between the houses.

Turn left into Coombe Street, walk a short distance down the hill and when you reach the parish notice board pass through the kissing gate into the field on the right signposted, Bourton ¾. Walk to the kissing gate on the far side, then bear left across the field making for the stile in the hedge on the far side. Climb over onto the drove track and turn left. Widening to a tarred surface the road drops gently to the T junction at which point turn right then left into the main road walking the short distance uphill to the pub.

Ecgberht's Stone

The Gaggle of Geese, Buckland Newton

Located high up in the Blackmoor Vale the Gaggle of Geese is a homely inn tucked well away in the small peaceful village of Buckland Newton. It was originally a shop built about one hundred and fifty years ago. The last time the inn changed hands was in 1987. The resident owners, Trev and Jan Marpole are no strangers to the licensed trade having previously run the Eclipse Inn in Winchester where they built up a very good reputation for food. Since taking up residence here they have carried out several improvements one of which included the removal of old decor from the bar to reveal an original stone wall and fireplace. There is just the one main bar with a separate games room at the rear, a skittle alley and large attractive garden.

The well stocked bar in this freehouse includes two regular real ales, Wadworth 6X and Badger Best plus a couple of guest ales.

A wide range of food is available both at lunch time and in the evening. There are the usual bar snacks such as sandwiches and various ploughman's plus a good selection of main meals. Typically to start there might be smoked mackerel, pate or homemade soup of the day, followed by various grills, fish dishes, pizzas and vegetarian meals. The sweet list usually includes homemade apple pie.

Children are very welcome.

Weekday opening times are from 12 noon till 2.30 p.m, or thereabouts and again from 6.30 p.m. until 11 p.m.

Telephone: (01300) 345249.

> God made the wicked grocer
> for a mystery and a sign,
> That men might shun the awful shops
> and go to inns to dine.
> *G. K. Chesterton*

17

Walk No. 6

Village signed from the B3143 north of Dorchester at the end of the Piddle Valley.

Approx. distance of walk: 3 miles OS Map 194 ST 688/050.

There is a large car park beside the inn also room in the lane outside.

A very pleasant, scenic walk mostly on tracks and open farm land which takes you high up and across the Knoll.

From the pub go left, past the telephone kiosk and take the first turning on the left. A short distance later, after passing a house look for a driveway on the left signposted, to Dominey's Yard. Walk up to the thatched cottage, bear right past a garage and then left through a wooden gate into a small field. Go across to the stile in the hedge opposite keeping straight ahead to the gate then turn left down to a gate in the hedge. Head up the field opposite making for the gate in the top right-hand corner turning right into the lane.

Upon reaching the hamlet of Henley turn left, carefully cross the main road and head up the track opposite forking right. Half way up there is a gate on the right, pass through into the field and bear half left towards a projecting corner of hedge and continue in the same direction, up and over the brow of the hill down to the stile in the hedge. Cross into the field and keep straight ahead, over the wire fence bearing right, up the bank and down towards a gate in the opposite hedge.

Follow the grassy track up to a couple of gates, through into the meadow and bear left walking round the hillside to a gate on the far side. Pass through, turn right and descend the very steep bank to the stile located in the hedge at the bottom, close by is a second leading into the field ahead after which head down and across to the stile in the field boundary turning left into the lane.

Keep walking and where the road dips look for a stile in the right-hand hedge then cross into the copse. Walk up to the gate and bear right over to the stiles, into the field and turn left walking to the gate at the top. Turn right onto the track and almost immediately take the signed footpath on the left. After crossing the back garden to the stile continue ahead to the stiles opposite and across to the gate. Bear half left across the field making for a pair of stiles in the side hedge and maintain your direction crossing a couple more stiles before bearing right over to the farm gate then up to the lane and turn left.

Cross over to the kissing gate following the well worn path to a similar gate, finally across to a metal gate, out into the lane and turn right. Take the next left back to the pub.

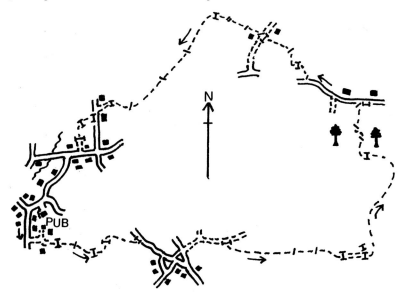

The Saxon Inn, Child Okeford

Tucked peacefully away behind cottages in Gold Hill is the delightful Saxon Inn. Originally three farm cottages built two to three hundred years ago it only became a pub in the early 1950's and was known at that time as The New Inn. It is an ideal family pub away from traffic hazards and having a large rear garden with a collection of farm animals which includes a Vietnamese pot belly pig that thinks it's a dog!

The main bar is simply but comfortably furnished with a large open fire whilst the lounge has a low beamed ceiling, part panelled walls and heated by a warm log burning stove. There are farm house tables and chairs on the carpeted floor, high back wooden settles against the walls where old prints and early photographs of the village can be viewed.

The inn is a freehouse well run for the past ten years by the present owners Roger and Hilary Pendleton. Three well conditioned real ales presently available are Butcombe Bitter, Draught Bass plus a guest ale.

A very good menu is offered and available all week, except Sunday evening and Tuesday evening. Snacks include sandwiches, toasties, five different ploughman's and jacket potatoes. The main menu lists homemade soup and deep fried Brie followed by traditional favourites like shepherds pie and homemade steak and kidney pie also curry, jumbo sausages, breaded plaice, scampi, steaks, ham, egg and chips and Dorset pork chops. Vegetarians are well catered for and there is a separate childrens' menu.

Weekday opening times are from 11.30 a.m. till 2.30 p.m. and 7 p.m. till 11 p.m.
Families are welcome in the lounge and dogs on a lead.
Telephone: (01258) 860310

Walk No. 7

Child Okeford is signposted beyond Shillingstone from the A357, Blandford to Sturminster Newton road. When you reach the village turn left at the road junction and continue past the centre. The inn is on the right off Gold Hill well hidden behind cottages.

Approx. distance of walk: 3¾ miles OS Map 194 ST 829/135.

Park in the road at the front, or the car park at the inn.

A lovely scenic walk up onto Hambledon Hill, site of an ancient Neolithic camp considered by many to be one of the finest examples in Southern England. For a longer walk you can combine this one with the walk from Shroton on page 79 joining it at the trig. point.

Turn left from the inn and left again into Ridgeway Lane. Metalled for a short distance the surface is soon gravel and mud. Some way ahead the track bears to the right (ignore the path ahead) but keep walking until you eventually reach the road at the top then turn right.

In about 300 paces turn left into the gravel drive and further ahead continue along the narrow path to the left of the entrance gates. It is a very attractive but often muddy, deep sided gully, shaded by an overhead canopy of hazel and home to a variety of ferns. At the top pass through the gate and keep straight ahead across the field until you reach the corner of an enclosed field at which point turn right and follow the grass track beside the boundary fence, up to and through the gate onto the bridleway.

Bear right up the bank and then left following the bridleway signs which lead you up onto Hambledon Hill. This impressive Iron Age fort dates from the 1st and 2nd century B.C. The path eventually reaches a gate beyond which is a fenced path leading

to the trig. point. Go through the gate on the right and, bearing right walk down the hillside to pick up the track. Follow it down through the gate into the field and then through the metal gate. The track passes beside woods on the left before reaching the road.

Turn right and immediately go over the stile into the field, and bear left up to the stile then bear right to the stile in the fence at the top. Cross the track and stile opposite and continue beside the hedge until a stile allows access down to the road.

Walk straight across into the drive of the house opposite, through the gate then through the gate on the left following the narrow path down to a small gate leading into an open field. At the bottom is a similar gate beyond which a short path leads down to an often wet and muddy area and stream. Go over the stile and up the field, over the crossing point into the field on the left and straight ahead to a stile, across a small field and one last stile following the grass track up to the road, turning right back to the pub.

The Barley Mow, Colehill

The Barley Mow is a part thatched two-storey inn probably built originally as a drover's cottage around the 16th century. It is one of my favourite inns in a beautiful country setting surrounded by fields. The lovely atmospheric main bar has a low beamed ceiling, panelled walls and a delightful inglenook fireplace with bread oven housing a warm winter log fire. The other bar has recently been extended to include a new fireplace with wood burning stove, the work sympathetically carried out with genuine old beams, bricks and flagstones and now blending perfectly with the older part of the building. At the back is a secluded terrace and large beer garden with childrens' play area and boule pitch.

The inn is owned by Hall & Woodhouse and very well run by Sue and Bruce Cichocki. The well stocked bar includes two real ales, Dorset Best Bitter and Tanglefoot.

Very good food is served seven days a week the set menu supplemented by the daily specials board. Their traditional homemade country cuisine is cooked in the old fashioned way, one of their specialities being pies topped with short crust pastry. They include poachers with venison and rabbit, hare and pheasant, turkey and mushroom and steak and kidney cooked in Guinness. Also listed are various chicken dishes such as Cotswold chicken - chicken filled with Stilton and wrapped in bacon, Cajun chicken and coriander and lemon chicken.

Weekday opening times are from 11 a.m. till 3 p.m. and 5.30 p.m. till 11 p.m.

Families are welcome.

Telephone: (01202) 882140.

Walk No. 8

This remote and beautifully situated inn is best reached from the Holt turning off the Ferndown by-pass then left at the Broomhill crossroads.

Approx. distance of walk: 3½ miles. OS Map 195 SU 032/023

The inn has its own large car park plus an overspill when busy, also a small lay-by at the front.

This very enjoyable country walk, ideal for families and which includes a nature trail, follows a series of field paths, a woodland path, bridleway tracks and peaceful country lanes.

From the inn turn right across the Green where you will find a gap in the hedge signposted, Lonnen Road. Cross the ditch climbing the stile into the field and walk straight across to the stile and plank bridge in the hedge opposite. Maintain your direction across to another stile, go over onto the bridleway and turn left. The bridleway route is behind the barn but often blocked so continue ahead towards the farm buildings turning right at the large painted footpath sign. Pass through the farmyard to re-join the bridleway and walk up to the road.

Go straight across, through the gate opposite and follow the track, over the river and through the gate into the field. Keep straight ahead through the gate opposite walking beside the hedge and ditch and up to the stile. Cross the track and head up the field to the stile and continue ahead close to the fence on the left. Upon reaching the stile cross into the adjoining field and bear left following the wire fence downhill and over another stile. At the bottom cross the stile and plank bridge then bear right, past the recently constructed ponds making for the crossing point in the hedge. Go over the bridge into the field, turning left and make for the stile then turn immediately right, over the concrete bridge and bear right up across the field to the gate, go out into the lane and turn right.

Keeping to the right-hand side, walk along the lane for a short distance turning left into Sheepcroft Lane. Go to the end of this gravel road then using the stile or gate enter the field on the left. Keep straight on to a similar gate and stile making for the

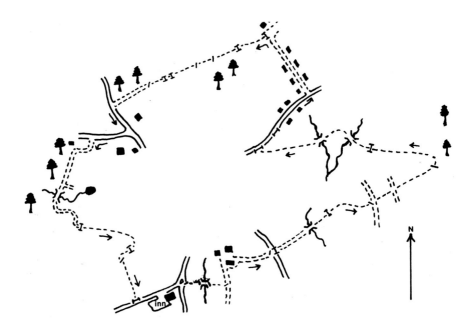

stile ahead. Maintain direction over a series of stiles leading to a wood. Follow this very attractive path up to the lane and turn left.

Carefully walk up the hill, turning right into God's Blessing Lane so named, it is said, because Cromwell's men, who were billeted near by, were blessed before the siege of Corfe Castle. Walk along the verge, past the entrance to Stewarts Nursery and look for the signed path on the left. Keep to the nature trail which passes a series of interesting fact boards then fork right across the wooden bridge. The path winds its way round a hedged and fenced field, home to many wild orchids, before turning into a field. Keep straight ahead walking almost to the far hedge then turn right through the gateway, (waymarked) up the field and upon reaching the pair of stiles cross into the adjoining field. Walk to the gate opposite, go out into the lane and turn left back to the pub.

Key to Symbols

════ road	----- track	---------- undefined path
/ stile	bridge	⊢—⊣ gate
gap in hedge		cattle grid

A section of the nature trail

The Fox Inn, Corfe Castle

Dating back to 1568 this small inn, reputed to be the oldest in Dorset, is totally in character with is ancient surroundings. From the street you enter directly into the small front bar, dominated by a large wooden table and wooden benches around the walls. There is a small serving hatch in the wall and an open winter fire. A narrow passageway leads through and down to the recently extended rear bar and lounge. During the work a well was discovered under the floor and is now an attractive feature viewed through a glass panel. There are good views from the delightful flower filled back garden with seating for up to 80 people.

The inn is a freehouse owned since 1990 by the licensees, Annette Brown and Graham White; Annette herself being born in the pub. Perfectly conditioned real ale is still served traditionally straight from casks in the bar. There is usually a choice of four such as The Bishop's Tipple, Wiltshire Traditional Bitter and Burton Ale.

Very good home-cooked, generously portioned bar snacks, available from 12 noon till 2 p.m. and 7 p.m. till 9.30 p.m. include tasty homemade soup, filled jacket potatoes, large rolls and sandwiches. You might also see listed steak and kidney pie, lasagne, delicious home-cooked ham with egg and chips, a pint of prawns, plaice fillet and battered mushrooms with a salad and garlic dip. Daily blackboard specials might include pork steak with garlic and mustard sauce or chicken and broccoli bake. Vegetarians are well catered for and there is always a good choice of homemade sweets.

Children in the garden only.

Weekday opening times are from 11 a.m. till 3 p.m. (2.30 in the winter) and from 6 p.m. (6.30 p.m. in the winter) till 11 p.m.

Telephone: (01929) 480449.

Corfe Castle is situated on the A351, Wareham to Swanage road. Turn right into the village centre then left. The inn is on the right.

Approx. distance of walk: 3¼ miles OS Map 195 SY 960/820.

There is no parking at the pub but from October 15 through till May 1 parking restrictions are lifted in the street at the front; at other times there is space in the square, a small lay-by opposite or the public car park further down the street.

An interesting, scenic walk through this attractive and historic village which guides you along bridleways and footpaths to the village of Church Knowle then back across farm land. Although easy going some paths can become very muddy in the winter.

Turn left from the pub then left into the cul-de-sac by the castle entrance. Go through the gate in the corner and follow the path around the castle turning left into the lane at the bottom. Cross the bridge, and in 50 paces climb the stile beside the gate on the right and take the bridleway track on the left signposted, to Knowle Hill. After rising steadily towards a gate, pass through and continue ahead, ignoring the paths off to the right. Pass through another gate following the footpath signposted, to Cocknowle. On the right is an old lime kiln once used extensively to burn limestone chalk to produce lime.

Further ahead cross the stile and then go over the stile on the left signposted, to Church Knowle. The grass path leads to a track which emerges beside the church of Saint Peter's dating back to 1225. Turn right into the lane, and after rounding the bend take the stony track on the left signposted, to Swyre Head via West Orchard. Where the track dips continue ahead in the direction of the waymark ignoring the track on the left.

At the end of the track pass through the farm gate and walk down the field to meet the stream at the bottom. Turn left and, keeping the stream on your right, walk across the field to the stile, into the field ahead and maintain direction across to the stile on the far side. Follow the path through the thicket, then across the drive and stile into the field opposite. Continue ahead close to the stream and, after passing through the gateway bear left, up and over the rise across to the gate in the corner. Keep straight ahead towards the wooden crossing point and follow the track down to the gate, cross the stream and climb the bank, pass through the gate bearing right across the field until you reach the small gate on the far side. Cross the bridge onto Corfe Common and follow the path ahead, up to the kissing gate then straight ahead towards the car park leaving by the stile. Turn left then left into the street walking the short distance up through the village and back to the pub.

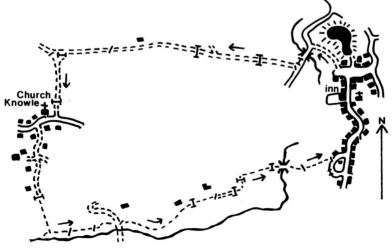

The Coventry Arms, Corfe Mullen

Dating back to the 15th century the inn was originally known as The Cock and Wheatsheaf and was the centre of village life until the villagers moved to the top of the nearby hill. When the inn was re-roofed a cat's skeleton was found nailed to the rafters following an old medieval tradition; it can be seen today in a glass case by the bar. Until 1990 there were just two small bars and a snug. The public bar was extended and is now predominantly a dining area with a servery at the rear. The lounge bar was enlarged slightly and opened up with the Pickwick room to provide additional seating. During the alterations the small coal fireplace was removed to reveal the original inglenook fireplace now with a warm log effect gas fire. The work was well done, the inn loosing nothing of its original character. Beyond the back terrace the garden leads down to the river bank where more picnic benches have been provided.

The inn is owned by Greenalls and well run by the licensees Simon & Nikki Trevis. Beautifully conditioned temperature controlled real ales are still served traditionally from barrels at the back of the bar. There are usually five which includes Ringwood Best and Old Thumper.

A good choice of freshly prepared home-cooked food is available during the week from 12 noon till 2 p.m. and 6.30 p.m. till 9.30 p.m. (Sunday 7 p.m. till 9 p.m.) Apart from the usual sandwiches and ploughman's meals on the printed menu include savoury calamari and Camembert with cranberry followed by lamb Provencal, rack of ribs, beef Wellington and the Coventry Arms chilli special - hot beef chilli on a bed of rice topped with melted Cheddar cheese served with garlic bread, coleslaw and a side salad. On a recent visit the specials board listed two grilled mackerel with a Mediterranean sauce and Somerset pork in a cider and cream sauce. Vegetarians and children are well catered for.

Families welcome.

Weekday opening times are from 11 a.m. till 2.30 p.m. (3 p.m. Saturday) and 5.30 p.m. till 11 p.m. All day opening only at busy times in the summer and Christmas.

Telephone: (01258) 857284.

The inn is beside the A31 Wimborne to Dorchester road just outside Wimborne.

Approx. distance of walk: 4 miles OS Map 195 SY 976/985.

There is parking at the side and rear of the inn and space in the lane by the church.

An enjoyable, easy going walk which explores a once rural area fast becoming urbanized. Good underfoot the walk is along pretty country lanes, on established paths, across farm land and through a small wooded area at Happy Bottom.

Leave the pub and carefully cross the busy trunk road into Brickyard Lane opposite. After passing the lane on the left and just beyond the clay pit take the gravel lane on the left. In fifty paces go through the gate into the field on the left and bear right up to the stile in the far top corner. Climb into the field keeping straight ahead down to the stile at the bottom.

Cross the lane and walk up the stony drive opposite, through the farm gate and straight ahead following the grass track. Pass through the yard between the buildings and bear right onto the tarred drive. When you reach the road turn left and then right into Haywards Lane. At the top turn left into Orchard Lane, walk down to the bottom and straight ahead onto the narrow gravel path. Follow it round and up past the church to meet the road at the top.

Turn right, cross over and go up the gravel lane on the left turning right at the house onto the tarred path and out into the cul-de-sac. Walk out to the road and turn right, cross over and follow the tarred path through the new housing development.

Upon reaching the stile beside the gate go out onto the bridleway and turn left. Turn right into Merley Park Road, and in twenty paces turn left onto the path beside the bungalow. Cross the wooden bridge at the bottom and follow the path ahead, up the bank through the trees and eventually out into the unmade road at Happy Bottom.

Turn left into Pine Road, cross the lane into Wayground Road, and after entering the housing estate, turn left and then right onto the signed footpath between the dwellings. Go through the kissing gate and follow the track ahead across the field. Pass through the gate into the playing fields keeping straight ahead until you reach the path down to the cul-de-sac. Turn right, and in one hundred paces look for a narrow tarred path on the right-hand bend by the street lamp, running beside No 19. At the bottom turn left and then right into the lane. Taking care as you go, walk down past the church turning left at the bottom back to the pub.

The Fox Inn, Corscombe

My first meeting with Martyn Lee was in 1988 shortly after he had purchased this charming, stone and cob, thatched 17th century inn; eight years on due to the dedication and hard work of both himself and his wife Susie The Fox is now firmly established as one of Dorset's premier inn's justly rewarded with one of only forty Egon Ronay stars countrywide and inclusion in The Good Food Guide.

Accommodation comprises two cosy, flag-stoned floored and beamed bars heated by open log fires, a pretty dining room and an attractive rear conservatory dominated by a massive oak slab table and draped with flowers. Candles and fresh flowers top the intimate tables whilst the gingham decor compliments the numerous hunting prints, stuffed birds, memorabilia and a interesting collection of cask taps.

The well stocked bar in this freehouse offers at least three well conditioned real ales presently Smiles Best Bitter, Exmoor Bitter and Fullers London Pride plus a very good wine list.

Excellent food, freshly prepared and cooked on the premises, caters for all tastes especially fish lovers. From a simple ploughman's or baguette the menu extends to fish soup, moules marinere and Fox's favourite - chicken in a cream sauce. The specials board on my visit listed squid in a rich Provencal sauce, scallops and turbot braised with mushrooms, wine and cream and Filipino style crab patties, followed by whole grilled lemon sole, fillet of sea bass with a fennel sauce, wild salmon with a sorrel sauce, roast rack of Dorset lamb, chicken liver salad and a red Thai chicken curry. Vegetarian meals include filo parcels filled with spinach, cream cheese and garlic and grilled aubergines baked with tomatoes, herbs and cream. No chips or microwave.

Well behaved children are welcome but no dogs in the bar.

Bed & breakfast will be available from 1997

Weekday opening times are from 12 noon till 2.30 p.m. extended at weekends and from 7 p.m. till 11 p.m.

Telephone: (01935) 891330.

Follow the A356, Dorchester to Crewkerne road for about 14 miles turning right shortly after the radio masts, the village and pub are signposted. Further on fork right at the road junction in the direction of Halstock.

Approx. distance of walk: 3½/4 miles. OS Map 194 ST 525/054.

Park in the lane or either car park.

An ideal walk for a fine summer's evening mostly across farm land and along peaceful green lanes. It is hilly and sometimes muddy in the winter but the views are spectacular.

Leave the pub turning right and in just a short distance turn left through the gateway opposite the road junction. Keep straight ahead cross the stream and pass through the gate into the field. Bearing slightly left walk to the far side following the well defined path, through the plantation and leave by the metal farm gate turning right into the lane.

Carry on past the water treatment plant and further ahead turn left at the track intersection following this green road steadily uphill to the village. Turn left, past a row of cottages and take the next turning right joining the track beyond the houses. After a steady climb between high hedges on an uneven and often wet surface one is soon rewarded with glorious views across the village to the distant hills. Upon reaching a wide wooden gate on the left join the 'permissive path' following it down and round the hillside past the Corscombe Stones (believed to be the site of a chambered long barrow) then through the gate to join the signed bridleway. Keep straight ahead past some standing stones then fork left towards the small metal field gate. In the direction of the arrow climb steeply to the top of the hillside, pass through the gate in the wire fence maintaining your direction across to the gate.

Cross to the gate opposite and bear left down the meadow and upon reaching the far side follow the fence turning right when you reach the gap. Bearing left descend the hillside making for a wooden gate in the far hedge (not the one you can see in the valley bottom but another higher up on the left). (For a slightly shorter walk keep fairly close to the hedge on the left, walk round to the farm gate in the bottom left-hand corner, enter the lane and turn left past the church turning right at the junction back to the pub). Otherwise keep straight ahead down the hillside close to woods on the right, pass through a gap in the hedge making for the metal gate beside the cottage.

Cross the track, go through the gate into the field and climb to the waymarked gap in the hedge, then bear left across to the stile, enter the lane and turn left.

One hundred and fifty paces later enter the farm on the right, pass between the buildings and join the track which doglegs left beyond the farm gate. Further on pass through the gate on the left and join the undulating green road down between fenced fields keeping straight ahead at the bend then down a narrow path and enter the field ahead. Bearing left head down to the gate, turn left into the lane then left at the junction back to the pub.

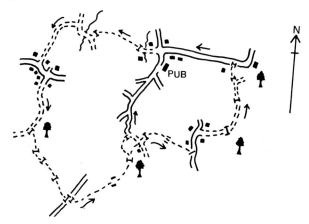

The Fleur de Lys, Cranborne

Historical records show that the Fleur de Lys was an inn as long ago as the 1600's but the building itself dates back to the 11th century. The cosy old-world charm of the inn owes much to this ancient origin. Friendly, warm and welcoming the comfortable wood-panelled lounge is tastefully decorated and heated in winter by a log burning fire in the large inglenook fireplace. There is small equally atmospheric public bar, and an attractive wisteria covered terrace at the rear.

It is an Hall & Woodhouse Inn under the personal supervision of Charles and Ann Hancock since 1977. There is an excellent wine list and two well conditioned real ales, Tanglefoot and Badger Best.

Over the years the pub has built a reputation for their excellent fayre priding itself on using only the freshest locally bought produce, fully justifying Egon Ronay's recommendation. Separate menus are available seven days of the week for both lunchtime and in the evening, with a blackboard in the lounge listing daily specials. Served between 12 noon and 2 p.m. and from 7 p.m. till 9.30 p.m. there are small bites, a choice of homemade specialities such as soups, steak pie, steak and kidney pudding, leek, lamb and apricot pie plus a variety of fish, grills and vegetarian dishes. The evening a la carte menu has a wide variation of dishes along with the hugely popular 3 course set meal which includes a glass of wine and coffee.

Weekday opening times are from 10.30 a.m. till 2.30 p.m. and 6 p.m. till 11 p.m. Sunday 12 noon till 2.30 p.m. and 7 p.m. till 10.30 p.m.

Children are welcome and well behaved dogs in the pub and garden.

Superior en-suite accommodation is available, with colour T.V., tea and coffee making facilities.

Telephone: (01725) 517282. Fax: (01725) 517631.

Pub situated opposite the Manor House in the centre of Cranborne on the B3078.

Approx. distance of walk: 4½ miles. OS Maps 195/184 SU 055/133.

Park in Castle Street at the side or in the pub's own car park but please refer to management before leaving your vehicle.

An easy and enjoyable scenic ramble from this most historic of Dorset towns. The going is mostly good underfoot on large wide tracks, across farm land and which passes through woods and the tiny hamlet of Boveridge.

From the inn turn right into Wimborne Street and further on left into The Square on the Boveridge road. Fork right and take the track on the left between two rows of houses. Pass through the small wooden gate and follow the track ahead leading to Manor Farm. Go through the metal gate and continue ahead along this tarred farm road for some distance until you reach Cranborne Dairy at which point take the signed bridleway on the right. Keep to this rather exposed but scenic grass centered track and upon reaching the bridleway enter the field ahead. Walk to the bottom, past farm buildings on the left then fork left up the track to meet the road.

Walk straight across towards Boveridge Farm, and after passing a pair of cottages on the left take the short track on the right towards the farm gate and immediately left onto the footpath beside the wood. You will notice clumps of evergreen butchers broom along the edge of the path which is often sprayed silver and used for decoration. Climb the wooden crossing point and walk to the stile at the bottom of the field following the narrow path thorough the trees, out into the lane and fork right towards Damerham. Just past a cottage there is a stile leading to a footpath on the right signposted, Burwood Pit ½. Good underfoot track rises steadily between a hazel coppice and young woodland then dips before rising to a gate.

Turn right into the road and almost immediately left joining the track along the edge of the field. Turn right on the far side then left into the cul-de-sac bearing left after which turn right to join the riverside path. Cross to the left at the car park and take the path up beside the school, into the road at the top turning right back to the pub.

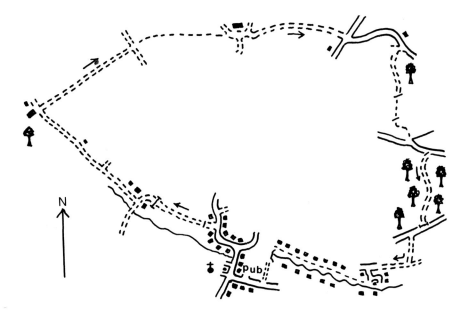

N

The Horns Inn, Deansgrove, Colehill

The Horns at Deansgrove is situated in a lovely rural location yet only minutes from the centre of Wimborne. Originally thatched this red-bricked inn is a picture in summer adorned with flower tubs and hanging baskets. Inside there are two comfortably furnished bars the larger mainly for dining. There is a side beer garden with picnic benches but my preference are those on the sunny front terrace.

On offer in this well run Hall & Woodhouse pub are two well conditioned real ales, Badger Best and Hard Tackle.

Reliably good home cooked food is served every day of the week. In addition to very good value sandwiches and ploughman's there is a comprehensive menu together with daily specials listed on the blackboard. To start there might be a tasty soup such as roasted red peppers with sweet corn, a bowl of pan fried mushrooms topped with melted Cheddar cheese, followed by 'odds-on-favourite' a 6 oz rump steak with oriental prawns in a light crispy batter, their famous ham platters for the large and smaller appetites, fresh Bridlington cod fillets, crispy coated deep fried plaice fillet, Galloping Major a prime horseshoe gammon, grilled and topped with egg or pineapple, Cajun chicken - a whole butterflyed chicken breast marinated in spices, grilled and served with ratatouille, pan fried mushrooms and a choice of potatoes, bangers in the rough and a vegetarian Kiev. Two homemade specialities include upper crust pie - flaky pastry pie filled with pieces of seasoned rump steak and mushrooms cooked in red wine and Desperate Dan pie made from best English braising steak and kidney slowly cooked in a rich gravy with Guinness.

Weekday opening times are from 11 a.m. till 2.30 p.m. and 6 p.m. till 11 p.m, Sunday 12 noon till 3 p.m. and 7 p.m till 10.30 p.m.

Telephone: (01202) 883557.

Leave Wimborne on the B3078 and after crossing Walford Bridge take the next right signposted, Burts Hill & Colehill.

Approx. distance of walk: 2¼ miles. OS Map 195 SU 018/0133.

Park at the front or beside the inn.

A short but pleasant walk in a lovely unspoilt area of Wimborne along peaceful country lanes and field paths. The going is easy underfoot except during the winter when certain areas can become wet and muddy.

Leave the inn turning left then right when you reach a gravel track, footpath waymarked. Beginning as a wide gravel track this attractive fenced path lined with holly trees rises steadily under a canopy of mature oaks. Fork left at the top and cross the road into Merrifield - a stony track which affords good views over the Stour Valley. Further ahead, after passing a couple of pretty thatched cottages, descend to the lane and turn right.

Keep to the lane for a short distance turning left into the driveway of Old Dairy Cottage signposted, Bothenwood and Dogdean Farm. Cross the stile into the field on the left and bear right following the boundary down to the damp crossing point in the bottom corner. Almost immediately turn left negotiating the plank bridges and stile and walk up the field keeping close to the hedge.

Upon reaching the stiles enter the adjoining field and turn right, through the gap in the hedge and up the field beside the hedge on the left. Climb the stile and continue ahead, crossing two more stiles before

reaching a stile on the left. Cross the drive and walk straight ahead keeping to the left of the wire fence. Maintain this direction over more stiles and wooden crossing points before finally following a narrow path beside a house leading to Smugglers Lane at which point turn right.

Walk to the T junction and, if not tempted to stop for a half way drink at the Stocks Inn, turn left into Furzehill. Keeping to the right-hand side of the road walk up the rise then down the hill, after passing a house named "The Rookery" cross the stile and join the signed footpath on the left. Narrow in places the path snakes between dwellings to a crossing point before running through the rear garden and out into the lane.

Turn left then take the path on the right signposted, Deans Grove. Cross the plank bridge and stile and head up the field keeping close to the hedge on the left. Negotiate the stile and continue walking up the field turning left into the lane at the top. Take the next right then right again back to the inn.

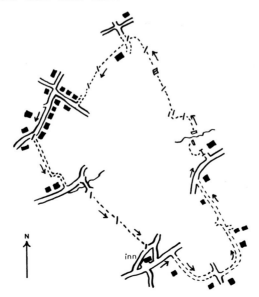

The Sailor's Return, East Chaldon

The name Chaldon means a hill where calves are pastured. The Herring family were Lords of East Chaldon in the 13th century when the village was much larger. Two of those early dwellings became The Sailor's Return - today an attractive, traditional 18th century inn. The name comes from the three brothers who went to join the navy, regrettably for their father only one was accepted, two returned so the father then converted his two cottages into an inn thus affording employment for them both.

Recent alterations have seen the addition of an attractive bar at one end and a stone walled dining room the other. The original bar remains much the same with solid walls, a flagstone floor and serving hatch in the wall.

Recently nominated for the title of 'Britain's Freehouse of the Year,' mentioned in the Good Pub Food Guide and Egon Ronay recommended, this beautifully kept inn is personally run by its owners who strive to provide the best of service in a friendly atmosphere. There is a very good range of real ales which presently include Wadworth 6X, Strong Country Bitter and from time to time Old Hookey, Old Speckled Hen and Exmoor Gold.

The menu is excellent and ranges from simple bar snacks, sandwiches, soup, filled French sticks and ploughman's through to one and a half pound local plaice, shell fish, poached salmon, duck, hocks, game and a variety of pies including steak and kidney, rabbit, ham and mushroom and fisherman's. All meals are homemade and the portions are large. In the words of the landlord 'The sailors returned and so will you'.

Children are welcome in the dining room.

Opening times are from 11 a.m. (Sunday 12 noon) till 2.30 p.m. and 6 p.m. till 11 p.m. (Sunday 10.30 p.m.)

Telephone: (01305) 853847.

Chaldon Herring or East Chaldon as it is more commonly known, is signed from the A352, Dorchester to Wareham road.

Approx. distance of walk: 6½ miles. OS Map 194 SY 791/834.

Park at the inn or in the village by the green.

A most enjoyable, scenic walk on bridleways, field and coastal paths and peaceful country lanes. Although fairly long it is not over demanding and mostly dry underfoot. For a shorter walk of about 2 miles however the Countryside Commission have an agreement with the Weld Estate through Vicarage Farm which extends to 1200 acres. Simply fork right up the track ignoring the signed path on the left then turn right at the farm buildings.

From the inn walk downhill to the village and bear left past the green onto the Winfrith Newburgh road. In a short distance turn right up the track signposted, to Daggers Gate. Pass through the gate and then a second. Keep walking until you reach the point where the track bears right and, unless you wish to do the short walk go through the farm gate on the left, along the grass track and through a couple more gates into a field. Continue ahead across to the gate following the track to the gate at the top of the field, beside farm buildings, across a couple more fields before reaching the road.

Turn immediately right onto the track signposted, to Ringstead & White Nothe. Further ahead go through the gate then through a couple more into a field. Keep straight ahead past four wooden sculptures representing four grains of wheat. Maintain your direction through another gate all the while climbing towards White Nothe. Along the path there are various stone sculptures set in the bank also a memorial stone to Llewelyn Powys - an author who lived in the village.

When you reach the junction of two paths climb the stile beside the gate and follow the signs to Ringstead. Further on pass through the gate, past a building and through a small gate into the field ahead. Keep to the track round the field until you eventually reach a stile beside a gate. Go over and a few steps further on pass through the gate onto the footpath signposted, to West Chaldon. After passing a barn a footpath sign directs you into a field on the right. The well trodden path crosses two fields before bearing left, up and then down to a gate. Walk down to a second gate and bear left to the track, pass through the gate at the bottom turning right into the lane walking a mile along this peaceful lane back to the pub.

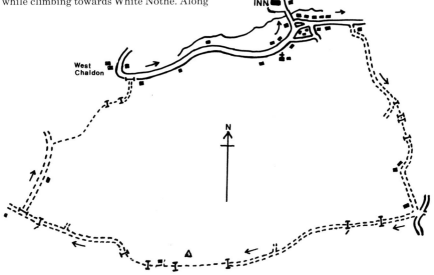

The Acorn Inn Hotel, Evershot

The Acorn Inn Hotel, nestling in this beautiful unspoilt peaceful village dates from the 16th century. It has inspired many not least Thomas Hardy who referred to the village as Evershead in Tess of the D'Urbervilles. Simply furnished the main bar has old flintlocks and stuffed birds on the walls and heated by an open log fire set in a stone fireplace, there is a small bar at the back with its own entrance and a separate beamed candlelit restaurant. There are a few picnic benches in the small rear garden.

A mecca for real ale lovers the choice on my last visit included Goldfinch Midnight Blinder, Munrows Mickey Finn, Fullers London Pride, Berkeley Lord's Prayer and Ringwood Old Thumper plus an excellent wine list.

Superb food, all freshly prepared, beautifully presented and efficiently served is available daily from 12 noon and up to 9.30 p.m. Apart from the usual snacks of sandwiches and ploughman's the daily specials board might list tasty homemade soup, venison, marinated herrings in Madeira, smoked meat platter, pigeon breast a la garlic and Madeira sauce, garlic mushrooms, game casserole, homemade steak and kidney pie, fresh fish parcels, cauliflower cheese, chicken curry, peppered beef - julienne of beef and peppers, stir fried vegetables, Thai prawns sizzler and sizzling duck with peach and ginger. Children and vegetarians are equally catered for as are sweet lovers who can choose between lemon zing trifle or hot toffee pancake with ice cream to name but two.

Overnight accommodation is available with a choice of four poster beds.

Dogs and families are equally welcome.

Opening times are from 11.30 a.m. till 2.30 p.m. (Saturday 3 p.m.) and 6.30 p.m. till 11 p.m. Sunday 12 noon till 3 p.m. & 7 p.m. till 10.30. p.m.

Telephone: (01935) 83228.

Evershot is signed from the A37 at Holywell north of Dorchester.

Approx. distance of walk: 6½ miles. OS Map 194 ST 573/045.

Ample parking at the front of the inn or in the rear car park.

This very scenic and fairly long walk, starting from Evershot one of many pretty villages set deep in this peaceful part of West Dorset, guides you first through the beautiful Melbury Park Estate, then through pretty Melbury Osmond (Thomas Hardy's Great Hintock) before reaching the Lewcombe Estate finally returning on field paths. Although generally good underfoot a few areas can become very muddy and challenging in places.

Turn left from the inn walking down to the green at the road junction. The standing stones, now built into a seat are, according to Peter Knight in his book, Ancient Stones of Dorset, believed to represent the three dumb sisters. Turn left here and enter the Melbury Estate. Cross the stile beside the cattle grid and continue through the park keeping straight ahead at the fork, through the metal gate and into the deer enclosure. There are usually plenty to be seen grazing on the surrounding lawns. Pass through a second gate and, when level with the house, turn left following the tarred drive ahead, through several gates before reaching the stile on the far side. A seat has been provided in the enclosure to rest awhile.

Turn right following the lane, into and up through the pretty and peaceful village of Melbury Osmond, crossing the bridge and turning left into the lane opposite Rock Cottage. The tarred surface soon narrows to a grass track leading to a farm gate. Keep going over a track and up to a pair of metal farm gates. Follow the gravel track ahead

which dips down between a woodland strip, across a bridge rising to a wooden gate. At the end of the track pass through the metal gate and keeping close to the hedge walk down to the bottom turning right and almost immediately pass through the small metal gate on the left. Often muddy and very uneven the narrow path drops steeply down through trees to a bridge at the bottom. Go through the gate keeping straight ahead, across the grass and up the bank to the small metal gate opposite. Keeping close to the hedge walk up the field making for the wide metal gate in the top corner. The attractive, rather lumpy and often muddy path beyond rises steadily past attractive woodland finally reaching the road at the top.

Turn left, walk for a while then turn left into the gateway of Lewcombe Manor, there

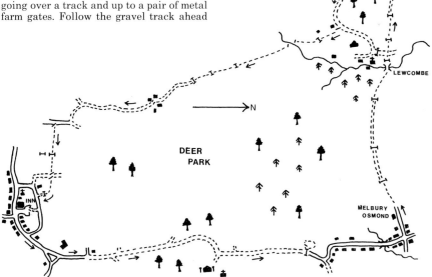

is a gate to the left of the cattle grid. Carry on down the tarred drive, through the gate beside the cattle grid and, after passing the cottage climb the stile into the field on the right. Cross in the direction of the waymark heading for the gate in the opposite hedge (presently green) then bear right down to the stile in the far right-hand corner. Go down the bank to the stream, carefully cross and climb the steep bank to the crossing point opposite.

Keep straight ahead in the field gradually drawing nearer to the hedge on the left. Upon reaching the far hedge pass through the gate into the field ahead and make for the gate opposite bearing right in the field, up to the metal farm gate and through onto the track. Just before reaching Girt Farm, climb the stile into the field on the left walking behind the buildings and out through the gate turning left onto the tarred drive. Climbing steeply up this drive take time to look back and enjoy the glorious Dorset scenery. Bear right at the top walking until you reach the stile on the left.

Enter the field and go down to the far hedge where there are two gates. Enter the field on the left, walk down to the stile, over the track and stile and into the field ahead. Bearing right make your way down to the bottom right-hand corner and just before reaching the dwelling turn right at the boundary hedge, pass through the gate, go down to the lane and turn left. A short distance ahead look for a narrow path on the right which leads straight to the rear car park of the pub.

Melbury Osmond

Melbury Park

The Museum Hotel, Farnham

The Museum dates back to Cromwellian times its name derived from the local museum established by the Pitt-Rivers family. Although having a more modern exterior, its age is obvious once inside. Tastefully decorated the 'Coopers Bar' with its large inglenook fireplace and original bread oven is heated by a warm log fire in a smaller fireplace whilst the 'Woodlands Bar' has a selection of pub games. There is a beautiful conservatory at the rear, a cosy candlelit restaurant and a pretty summer terrace and beer garden. What remains of the village stocks can still be seen at the front.

The inn is a freehouse extremely well run for the past eleven years by the owner John Barnes. For lovers of real ale there is always at least a choice of four.

The Museum offers a very good and imaginative choice of lunch time snacks ranging from homemade soups like carrot and coriander, fresh oysters, scrambled eggs with smoked Scotch salmon or herrings Swedish style also baked summer vegetables, fresh asparagus omelette and a saute of kidneys and bacon. Typical evening specials might include smoked salmon with a duet of pears or grilled tiger prawns with bacon followed by grilled Dover sole, breast of duck sweet and sour and a rack of lamb with flageolet. For afters try the fresh figs with cream if on the menu or maybe hot fresh pineapple with Kirsch. All food is beautifully presented especially the salads.

Families are welcome in the dining room or conservatory.

Accommodation is available in the converted stable block.

Weekday opening times are from 11 a.m. till 3 p.m. and 6 p.m. till 11 p.m.

Telephone: (01725) 516261.

Walk No. 16

Farnham is well signed from the A354, Blandford to Salisbury road at its junction with the Horton road.

Approx. distance of walk: 4 miles OS Maps 184 & 195 SU 957/151.

The inn has a good car park at the rear but there is ample space in the village.

Almost every cottage is thatched in Farnham a delightful, unspoilt working village in peaceful rural Dorset. This very enjoyable, scenic walk takes you across open farm land, along attractive bridleways and peaceful country roads. Whilst generally good underfoot some paths can become overgrown in summer.

From the pub turn right then immediately right again at the telephone box towards Chettle. Walk up the hill past the Old Rectory and Museum cottage then join the signed footpath on the left. Climb the bank to the stile and cross the field to the stiles opposite. Maintain direction to the pair of stiles ahead then continue beside the hedge, across the field to the stiles and stepped bank down to the road.

Walk straight across beside the electricity sub-station, through the small gate and bear left down the field making for the gate in the far hedge. Follow the bridlepath past the copse into the back garden of the dwelling, across the lawn to the gate and out into the lane turning right towards the hamlet of Minchington.

Just before reaching a thatched cottage cross the plank bridge and stile and enter the field on the left. Keep straight ahead to the gate, across the track and follow the sunken path up the hillside. When you reach the top of the field pass through the gate on the right and join the narrow track

ahead between the fields. Pass through a similar gate and continue walking for quite some distance, ignoring the stile on the right. Eventually the bridleway merges with a wide farm track, passes between farm buildings then rises steadily, before crossing a field to the road.

Cross over and turn left. There are no pavements and only a narrow grass verge so walk with care. Go past the entrance to Rushmore Park Golf Club and the Rushmore Estate, continue downhill and take the next left signposted, Farnham 1¼. Keep straight ahead up the hill and, after passing the small wood enter the field on the right by the waymark post.

Keeping close to the hedge on the right walk round until you reach a large oak and can clearly see the village then bear left across the field to the stile in the hedge opposite. Continue ahead behind the houses on the right, under the power cables and make for the farm gate, go out into the lane and turn left down through the pretty village to the pub.

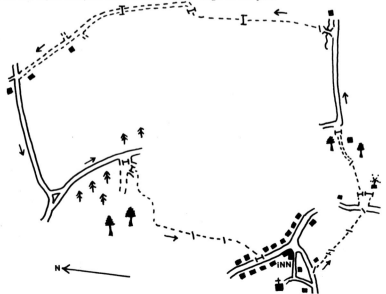

N ←

40

The Fiddleford Inn, Fiddleford

The Fiddleford Inn, a two-story, creeper-covered stone building dates back to around 1740. In its time it has also been a malt house and an old coaching stop. It last changed hands in 1990 and the owners, Jane and Lester Wareham immediately set about refurbishing the interior and a very good job they made of it. During the work many original features were discovered including the stone walls and flagstone floor. A warm log fire in the central fireplace heats both bars in winter. There is also a separate attractive dining room. Outside at the front is a lawned beer garden with a barbecue.

A good range of real ales presently available in the well stocked bar of this freehouse presently include Theakston XB and Old Speckled Hen.

Food is freshly prepared and served seven days a week. Apart from snacks which include substantial ploughman's, jacket potatoes and sandwiches the specials board might list salmon steak poached in white wine, rabbit and leek pie and pork and apple sausages. The main menu offers several light bites and starters which include homemade soup, a delicious pancake filled with prawns, white fish and mushrooms in a cream sauce topped with melted cheese, farmhouse breakfast, whole giant prawns served cold with mayonnaise or hot with garlic butter followed by various grills, homemade steak and kidney pie, homemade fish pie, fillets of beef pan fried with Scotch whisky, lamb cutlets with a tangy orange and Cointreau sauce and Mediterranean chicken - the breast served with a homemade sauce of tomatoes, onions, garlic and herbs. Vegetarians are well catered for with dishes like a vegetable curry or an aubergine and bean casserole and there is a good choice of childrens' meals. Sweets range from homemade Dorset apple cake to a fruit pie or crumble.

Children are welcome in the dining room but no dogs.

Weekday opening times are from 11 a.m. (winter 11.30 a.m.) till 2.30 p.m. and from 6.30 p.m. (winter 7 p.m.) till 11 p.m.

Telephone: (01258) 472489.

Walk No. 17

Fiddleford is a small village on the main A357 between Blandford and Sturminster Newton. The inn is just set back from the road.

Approx. distance of walk: 5 miles. OS Map 194 ST 805/132

Park in the lane at the front or in the car park of the pub.

A most enjoyable and interesting scenic walk ideal for spring or early summer which first takes you along an attractive riverside path towards Fiddleford Mill and Manor, through a bluebell wood and later enters the small village of Hammoon. Slightly demanding but generally good underfoot the walk follows established bridleways, field paths and country lanes.

Turn right from the pub down the lane and soon join the signed footpath on the left. Follow this very attractive riverside path, back out into the lane and straight ahead towards Fiddleford Mill. Cross the bridge and turn left. Fiddleford Manor on the right is open from the 1st April till 30th September daily from 10 a.m. till 6 p.m. and from 1st October till 31st March from 10 a.m. till 4 p.m. Carry on up the lane to the road turning right.

Carefully cross over and join the bridleway opposite signposted, Broad Oak 1. The narrow track rises steadily through a bluebell wood to meet a cross track at the top. Turn right following this well beaten track through the trees turning left at the next cross track by the fingerpost signposted, Angers Lane & Fiddleford. Further on climb the wooden crossing point over the deer fence, pass through the plantation and leave by a similar crossing point. Keep straight ahead down through the trees to the stile and into the field. Bearing left go down to the bottom of the field, through the gap in the hedge and continue down keeping close to the fence on the right. Cross the ditch, walk up to the stile, go out into the lane and turn left.

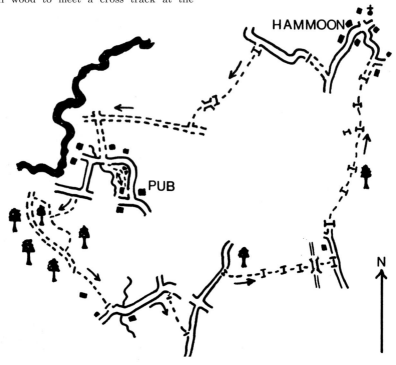

HAMMOON

PUB

N

Having reached the main road turn right along the verge and in a few steps join the signed footpath on the right. Climb the bank to the stile and head up to the top of the field keeping close to the hedge on the right. Cross the stile into the lane and turn left. Keeping to the right-hand side of the road walk down to the main road and carefully cross over into the lane opposite towards Hammoon.

Upon reaching the signed bridleway on the right, pass through the gate into the field and bear left down to the gate in the far corner. Keep straight ahead beside the hedge, through a couple of gates then pass under the bridge and out through the gate into the lane turning left.

Walk past the dwelling, through the metal gate and up the field bearing right at the top. Keep straight ahead through the gate, past Diggers and Ham Down copse on the right and maintain direction through a couple more gates. With the hedge on your left walk to the far side and go through the gate

on the right. Pass through two more gates, follow the track up to the lane and turn left.

Walk round to the centre of Hammoon turning left at the crossroads opposite the 14th century church of St. Paul's. Hammoon takes its name from 'Ham' meaning a dwelling and from 'Mohuns', its ancient lords of the manor. What remains of the Hammoon Cross can be seen at the junction after being re-erected by Alfred Pope in 1913. After leaving the village keep walking up the lane until you eventually come to a signed bridleway on the right.

Proceed along this well surfaced gravel track, through the gate, turning left then right, and upon reaching the gate enter the field on the left. Cross to the small red gate in the far left-hand corner, go over the bridge into the field and bear left up the bank onto the old railway line and turn right. Turn left at the cross track and upon reaching the lane either re-trace your steps back to the pub along the path beside the stream or keep to the lane.

Fiddleford Manor

43

The Crown, Fontmell Magna

Dominated by its 15th century church Fontmell Magna is one of several Dorset villages which still boasts a village local. Small but attractive a warm and friendly atmosphere pervades throughout The Crown which dates back to the 1800's and was once part of the brewery next door. The main bar, separated by a cartwheel divide, is decorated with a collection of mirrors, old photographs and tapestries collected by the licensees since they took over in 1980. The pub also has a small simply furnished public bar and beer garden which includes a boule court. Morris men can often be seen dancing in the large car park at the front. Perhaps the most unusual feature is Fontmell Brook which meanders through the pub and requires a crossing via a picturesque bridge to reach the pub toilets. Rising at Seven Springs, in the grounds of The Springhead Trust, the brook was first recorded in the 8th century and by 1085 served three corn mills and latterly powered the bottle machine factory which supplied the village brewery.

The well stocked bar in this Hall & Woodhouse pub offers traditional cider and three real ales namely Badger Best, Tanglefoot and I.P.A.

Good home-cooked food is available seven days a week with the main menu chalked daily on blackboards around the bar. Apart from Sunday when a wider choice of steaks are available typical daily fayre might include homemade soup, ploughman's, home-cooked ham, egg and French fries, homemade steak and kidney pie, homemade chicken curry with rice and Cumberland sausage. For vegetarians there are dishes like vegetable lasagne, vegetable sausage and mushroom and nut fettuccine. There are also childrens' specials.

Families welcome.

The Crown is open during the week from 11 a.m. till 2.30 p.m. and 6 p.m. till 11 p.m.

Telephone: (01747) 811441.

The pub is sited on the edge of the village on the A350 between Blandford and Shaftesbury.

Approx. distance of walk: 4½ miles OS Map 183 ST 867/169.

Park in the lane beside the inn or in the car park.

A most enjoyable, scenic walk circumventing the Fontmell Down Nature Reserve. Although fairly demanding in places the going is generally good underfoot but can be extremely muddy in one or two places during the winter.

From the pub carefully cross the main road into the lane opposite signposted, Ashmore 3. This peaceful lane rises steadily beside Fontmell Brook passing some very attractive cottages. Once beyond Springhead Farm take the next track on the left (path waymarked). Follow this often muddy, grass centered track up to the stile beside the gate and continue ahead to a another stile and gate entering Fontmell Nature Reserve. Acquisition of this 723 acre holding began in 1977 with the 148 acres of Fontmell Down purchased after a successful public appeal. During the summer up to 90 different plants can be seen along with 25 different butterflies. Keep to the wide woodland path which rises very steeply after which follow the narrow path bearing right up the hillside. Ignore the stile on the right but keep straight ahead to the stile beside the gate, cross over and keep straight ahead, ignoring the track on the left. Cut into the wooded

hillside this very attractive scenic path is home to numerous ferns and wild flowers. Pass through a gate and further on at the point where the track arcs to the right go to the left and follow the narrow hillside path ahead overlooking Longecombe Bottom. Cross the stile on the far side and bear left up across the hillside turning left upon reaching the wire fence. Keep to the top of the down until you reach the cross dyke at which point bear right then turn left along the fence. After a few steps cross the stile into the adjoining field and bearing left, walk steadily away from the fence, down the hillside to meet a grass track leading to a wooden gate. Pass through and keeping close to the wire fence on the left walk all the way round the field (ignoring the wooden crossing point on the left) until you eventually reach the small metal gate allowing access to the bridleway. Follow this very attractive sunken track between high

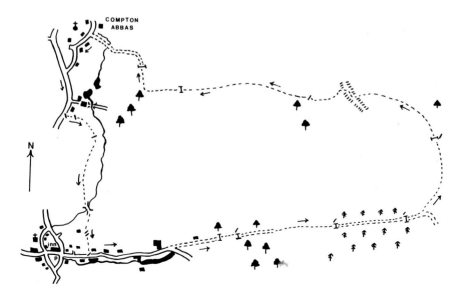

hedged fields then up beside a running brook turning left into the road at Compton Abbas. Keep bearing left through this pretty village, up to the main road, carefully cross over and turn left.

It is a busy road and there are no pavements so take care. After passing the driveway to Greenhayes Manor Farm look for a stile on the left, walk through the plantation and down to the copse at the bottom. To avoid some of the road there is a footpath further down the road on the right (waymarked). Bear right to stiles at the top of the field go through the gate on the left then turn left down the track to the road. Cross over into the playing fields and bear left down to the copse at the bottom. Follow the signed path through to the stile, climb into the field and turn right. Bearing slightly left make for the gap in the hedge on the far side and cross the bridge (can be extremely muddy). Bear left up the field keeping to the left of the barn where you will find a planked crossing point in the hedge, go into the field and cross to the stile on the far side, turning right into the lane back to the pub.

Compton Abbas

The Smith's Arms, Godmanstone

The Smith's Arms at Godmanstone, nestling in the heart of the beautiful Cerne Valley is a very quaint, thatched inn reputed to be the smallest in England. It was originally a blacksmith's shop granted a licence by Charles II in 1665. Apparently while hunting in the area the King called in and asked for a drink, when told there was no licence he granted one on the spot.

The pub's one small comfortable bar is well furnished, immaculately kept and heated by an open coal fire. All around the walls are lots of brightly shining copper and brass items and various memorabilia and photographs of the landlord's days as a jockey. There are picnic benches at the front with more on the lawn at the side - a lovely spot to sit in summer watching the ducks on the river and sheep on the surrounding hills.

The inn is a freehouse well run for a number of years now by the present owners Linda and John Foster. There is just the one well conditioned real ale, presently Ringwood Best still served traditionally straight from the barrel behind the bar plus house red and white wine.

Although small the inn offers a very good selection of bar food every day including Sunday. The majority of meals, home cooked on the premises, include tasty soup of the day such as cream of broccoli, curried parsnip or Stilton, homemade quiche and French bread, sweet pickle and salad garnish. In addition to the usual pub snacks such as jacket potatoes and sandwiches, plain or toasted, there are home cooked platters of beef or ham. Daily specials might include cod and prawn pie or homemade steak and kidney and to complete your meal tempting homemade sweets like bread and butter pudding, bakewell tart and peach flan.

Children and dogs are not permitted inside the pub.

Weekday opening times are from 11 a.m. till 3 p.m. and 6 p.m. till 11.00 p.m. The pub is presently closed for the whole of January each year.

Telephone: (01300) 341236.

Walk No. 19

Pub situated on the A352, 5 miles north of Dorchester.

Approx. distance of walk: $3\frac{1}{2}$ miles. OS Map 194 SY 667/974.

Park beside the pub or in the small lay-by opposite.

A most enjoyable, scenic walk in the beautiful Cerne Valley across farm land, along bridleways and beside the Cerne river. It is hilly but easy going and generally dry underfoot. An interesting area reached early in the walk contains several modern day sculptures.

Leave the inn and turn left keeping to the road for a short distance turning right when you reach Manor Farm, bridleway signed. Go up the track, through a couple of gates, then through a couple more before reaching the gate at the top. (A stile on the right allows access to a small enclosure containing stone sculptures erected by a local landowner).

Enter the field and turn left. Keeping close to the hedge walk to the gate on the far side and follow the track ahead, through a similar gate and maintain direction, past the trig. point in the hedge on the right and up to a gate at the end of the track.

Pass through and turn immediately left, through a similar gate and along the track passing a recently installed telecommuni-

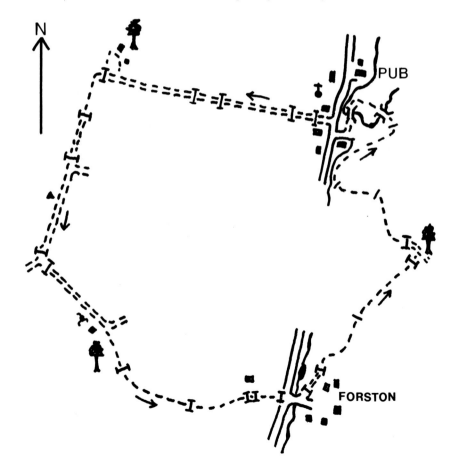

48

cations tower. Walk past the barn, enter the field and keep straight ahead close to the hedge and wood on the right walking until you reach a gate. Go through into the field and bear left following the well defined track down the hillside, through a gate gradually arcing left down the meadow then beside the hedge, through a couple of gates in front of the stables finally down to the gate and into the road.

Cross into the drive of Forston Farm and immediately go through the gate on the left following the drive past the farmhouse and through the gate into the field. Bear right along the track close to the river walking beside the hedge on the left and up to the farm gate. Passing through turn right and make your way up the field to the gate in the hedge in the top right-hand corner.

In twenty paces turn left through the gate and follow the well beaten grass track down the field until you reach a stile near the bottom on the left. Walk to the bottom of the field, cross the stile into the adjoining field and keep straight ahead close to the river until the inn is in sight. Cross the stile into the field on the left, go over the bridge, through the gate and round the mill into the road turning right back to the pub.

One of several stone sculptures you will encounter during the walk

49

The Drover's Inn, Gussage All Saints

This fine 16th century, part-thatched and tiled, brick built inn enjoys an isolated rural setting in a high sunny position with commanding views over the surrounding downs. Inside are two cosy, inter-connected bars both oozing with character. The larger has a low beamed ceiling and is dominated by a massive inglenook fireplace housing a warm winter log fire whilst the smaller has a part beamed ceiling and open fire. Furnishings consist of a mix of farmhouse tables and chairs. There are picnic benches on the sunny front lawn with more in the back garden also a childrens' play area with wendy house, swing bridge and platform.

The inn is a free house well run by the owner, Krystyna and manager Steve Collins. The well stocked bar includes country wines and a good selection of real ales such as Marston's Pedigree, Draught Bass, Ruddles Best plus additional beers guest beers from time to time.

The Drover's is a very popular and good place to eat offering not only a good choice of childrens' meals and snacks like ploughman's and homemade soup but an interesting selection of meals on the menu or listed daily on the specials board. Hotch potch mushrooms with sun dried tomatoes might proceed the curry of the day, gammon and eggs, roast rib of beef, veal in real ale, braised lambs liver in a red wine sauce with bacon and the popular Drover's steak and mushroom pie. Fish dishes might include halibut steak, supreme of salmon or smoked haddock with parsley butter and vegetarian dishes such as mushroom stroganoff and pasta with a cream, white wine and Stilton sauce. Tempting sweets range from deep treacle tart and homemade fruit crumble to chocolate and Tia Maria mousse and spirals of meringue filled with fresh cream served with chocolate or butterscotch sauce.

Families welcome.

Weekday opening times are from 11 a.m. till 2.30/3 p.m. and 6 p.m. till 11 p.m. Telephone: (01258) 840084.

The inn can be reached either from the A354, Dorchester to Salisbury road by taking the turning at Cashmoor signposted, Gussage All Saints, or from the Horton crossroads off the B3078 Wimborne to Cranborne road.

Approx. distance of walk: $4\frac{1}{2}$ miles. OS Map 195 SU 003/106

Park behind or at the front of the inn.

An easy walk on large wide tracks ideal for that family day out. It is especially pretty in springtime when numerous bluebells, primroses and cowslips line the route.

Head up the grassy track beside the pub (path signposted) pass through the farm gate and turn left to join a similar track. Continue ahead then fork left downhill turning right onto the gravel track at the bottom. The track then rises steadily past game woods on the left.

Ignore the smaller track on the right but maintain your direction along the grassy track running between the field and the edge of Harley Wood. Glorious in springtime this lovely bluebell wood is also home to the early purple orchid. Round the bend near the top ignoring the track on the left and continue on until you reach the cross track. Turn left, and a few steps further on turn left again and join the track beside Ackling Dyke, course of the old Roman road.

Amble along this track beside a large field until you reach a farm gate on the left in the corner of the field. Go through and, keeping close to the hedge on the right, walk to the far corner then pass through the gate on the right and follow the grassy track which skirts woodland on the left then heads to the right in the direction of the village. The track bears left at the bottom then meets a cross track at which point turn right passing through a couple of gates. There are two route options back to the pub. Either continue down past the church turning left into the village road or join the signed footpath on the left upon reaching College Farm. Turn left into the yard and keeping close to the hedge on the right walk up the driveway to the house and make for the right-hand corner then enter the field. Maintain your direction until you eventually reach a stile allowing access to the rear of the inn.

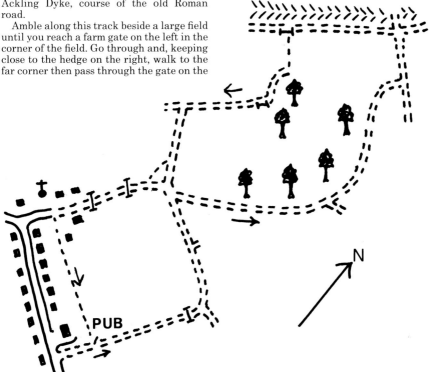

The Horton Inn, Horton Cross

The Horton Inn, originally an old 18th century coaching stop was the place Thomas Hardy had in mind as the rendezvous for his eloping heroine in the Old Surgeon's macabre story in The Nobel Dames collection. Today it is a comfortable inn with an excellent candlelit restaurant and well appointed bar with an open log fire. Outside tables, chairs and picnic benches are neatly positioned on the sunny front terrace.

A good selection of wines, two ciders and real ales, which presently include Ringwood Best and True Glory, Flowers and Directors Bitter, are always available in this freehouse.

There is an extensive bar menu supplemented with daily specials. The present menu lists garlic mushrooms, deep fried Camembert, moules marinere, smoked duck breast, warm beef salad followed by peppercorn pork, supreme of chicken, rack of lamb, supreme of salmon, fish medley, hunters porterhouse steak, noisettes of lamb. Vegetarians can choose between sweet pepper and mangetout stir fry served with honey and soy dressing and mushroom stroganoff.

The inn is open all day every day from 11 a.m. (12 noon Sunday) till 11 p.m. (10.30 p.m. Sunday).

Families are welcome.

Accommodation is available all bedrooms having tea making facilities and colour T.V.

Telephone: (01258) 840252.

The inn is situated on the B3078 at the Horton crossroads about 5 miles from Wimborne.

Approx. distance of walk: 5 miles. OS Map 195 SU 017/086.

There is a large parking area at the pub also a small area of verge opposite.

One of the most scenic walks in the area which takes you through the beautiful Crichel Park Estate where you have a good view of the house and lake and through the tranquil villages of Hinton Martell and Chalbury. Not over demanding the walk for the most part is on well surfaced tracks and farm land with short sections along the highway. Although mostly good underfoot certain areas can become very muddy in winter more especially the path up to Chalbury.

Leave the inn turning right, and keeping to the right-hand side of the road carefully walk down the hill, over the bridge and take the gravel track on the left beside the Stanbridge Pumping Station. Further on keep straight ahead through the gate steadily walking up this often muddy track. After passing the farm turn left at the cross track passing the mill. Further on cross the bridge and turn right, walk past the dwelling and keep straight ahead at the next junction turning right after passing the barn to join the attractive woodland path beyond the gate.

Cross the bridge, fork left over a second bridge keeping to the track ahead. During the hurricane many mature trees were lost but I am glad to see considerable new planting has taken place. Pass through the white painted kissing gate and along the track from which you have a good view of Crichel House across the lake. Turn left at the drive, past the playing fields, out through the gate house and turn left towards New Town.

Walk past all the cottages to the bottom of the village and join the narrow path at the back of the old Whitchampton Board Mill (shortly to be demolished and replaced with

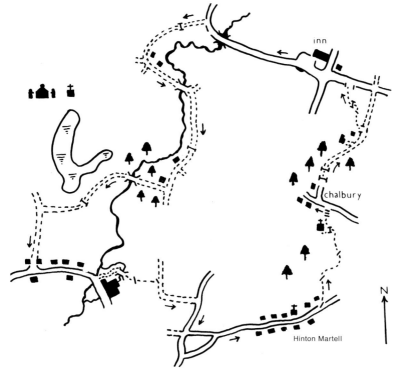

housing). Cross the stile into the field, walk to the one opposite and turn right following the grass tracked bridleway up to the road and turn right.

Keeping to the grass verge on the right walk until you reach the dwelling at which point cross into the lane opposite. Turn left at the road junction into the village of Hinton Martell. Fork left at the pond, up past the church climbing the hill until you reach the signposted footpath on the left.

Go up the bank to the stile, turn right and follow the fenced path steeply up the hillside, across a couple of stiles and into the field bearing right up to the stile near the top of the hedge on the left. The fenced path (often very muddy) skirts the field, dips to a plank bridge then rises to a stile. Cross the field to the stile, pass through the kissing gate into the churchyard, walk round to the front gate and turn left (good views).

Keep straight ahead along the road then almost immediately fork right signposted, Horton Inn $1\frac{1}{4}$. Walk down through the wooden gate then through a second gate into the wood. Keep to the main track, and after passing Chalbury Farm Cottages cross the stile into the field on the left. Either bear right across the field or walk round to the stile, climb into the adjoining field then over the pair of stiles into the field on the left. Bearing right go down to the stile in the far hedge turning left back to the pub.

Key to Symbols

———— road	- - - - - track	- - - - - undefined path
✔ stile	⟩—⟨ bridge	⊢—⊣ gate
⊣ ⊢ gap in hedge	⊟ cattle grid	

Hinton Martell

Drusilla's Inn, Horton

Drusilla's a pretty thatched, red-bricked inn was until 1978 a country tearoom. During the conversion 'The Tower Room', an attractive circular restaurant, was added. The south facing front bar has a low beamed ceiling and is heated by a log fire in an attractive inglenook fireplace whilst the rear 'Locals Bar' includes a pool table. There are benches on the lawn at the back but the most sought after seats are those overlooking the fields on the sunny front terrace. In 1995 it was voted 'Pub of the Year' by the local community.

The inn is a freehouse well run since 1993 by the owner Roger Kernan. The range of real ales include Flowers Original, Marston's Pedigree plus a guest such as Ringwood Bitter.

Very good food is offered all week plus a selection of fresh fish and speciality salads. The menu, which includes several baguettes with interesting fillings, ranges from firm favourites like steak and kidney pie to imaginative dishes like Chicken Piri - hot spicy chicken breast served on a bed of aromatic rice made to an African recipe. Blackboard specials might include homemade soup and mussels followed by poached salmon steak, shark steak 'au poivre', pan fried skate wing, half a pheasant casserole, Lancashire hot pot and vegetarian dishes like leek & Gruyere pie and spicy courgette and mushroom bake. Delicious puddings range from Dorset apple cake to traditional baked rice pudding. An a la cart menu is available every evening, also a junior choice menu is available.

Weekday opening times are from 11 a.m. till 3 p.m. and 5.30 p.m. till 11 p.m. Cream teas are available Sunday afternoons

Families are welcome.

Telephone: (01258) 840297.

Walk No. 22

The inn can be reached either from the A31 at Ringwood taking the Horton road at the Ashley Heath flyover or from Wimborne on the B3078 turning right at the Horton Inn.

Approx. distance of walk: 2½ miles. OS Map 195 SU 039/075.

There is a large car park at the rear of the pub. It is not possible to park safely in the road.

An interesting short, scenic walk across farm land, through bluebell woods and which passes beside the historical Horton Tower. The going is generally easy although a couple of areas can be slightly muddy in winter.

Leave the inn turning left, cross over and carefully walk up the road for a short distance until you reach the stile on the right. Climb into the field and walk down beside the hedge, cross the stiles into the adjoining field and turn left. Keeping close to the hedge walk round, through the farm gate and up to a small wooden gate leading into woods on the left. Pass through and almost immediately take the little waymarked path down into the bluebell wood on the right.

Follow it through the trees to the cross path on the far side at which point turn right. Many other wild flowers can be seen during the summer including purple orchids. Join the path out of the woods and up the field towards the tower. It was built in the 18th-century by Humphrey Sturt in order that he might watch the local deer hunt. Having fallen into disrepair it was recently taken over and restored by a communications company.

From the tower head down the field bearing left towards the village. Near the bottom cross the stile and metal gate and continue ahead across the field to the stile beside the

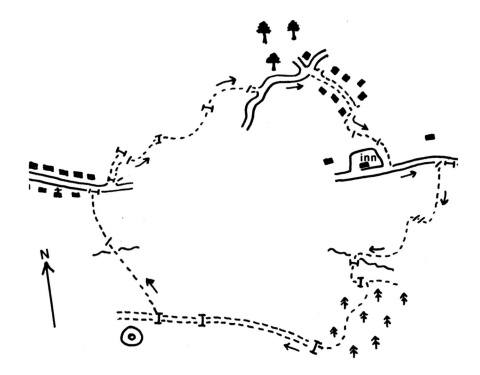

farm gate opposite the post office. Turn right along the Horton road, and after a short distance turn left onto the gravel track signposted, Haythorn.

Walk until you reach the stile on the right, climb into the field and go up to the gate in the hedge on the far side then make your way up the field to the stile at the top, out into the lane and turn left. Walk towards some properties on the left then turn right into the gravel road (there is a yellow waymark on the telegraph pole). Walk past all the houses and cottages to the wire fence at the bottom then turn right and follow the narrow path around the fields back to the pub.

The Horton Tower

The Crown Inn, Ibberton

The Crown is delightfully situated in the centre of Ibberton in a peaceful lane leading up to the church. Built sometime between the 15th and 16th century, the inn originally had just the one small bar, today there are two. The rear bar is mostly for dining whilst the main bar, which extends into a smaller cosy seating area, still has its original flagstone floor and is dominated by the large inglenook fireplace. Hanging from the mantel are three unusual Burmese prayer gongs collected by a previous landlord during his travels. Both bars are attractively decorated with lots of old photographs on the part panelled walls whilst furnishings consist of simple farmhouse tables and chairs. A small brook runs between the car park and the small lawned rear beer garden.

The Crown is a freehouse well run by the owners John & Linda Wild. There are two real ales served by hand pump Wadworth 6X plus a guest ale.

Good home-cooked food is served seven days a week, the menu chalked daily on the blackboard. Apart from the usual snacks of sandwiches, rolls and ploughman's you can choose chilli, jumbo sausages, chicken curry, various grills, chicken Kiev, omelettes and pies like steak & kidney and steak & mushroom. Sunday lunch is popular but you are advised to book first.

Children are welcome but no dogs.

Opening times can be flexible dependent upon trade but generally the hours are from 11 a.m. till 2.30 p.m. and 6 p.m. till 11 p.m. Sunday 12 noon till 3 p.m. and 7 p.m till 10.30 p.m.

Telephone: (01258) 817448.

Peacefully situated beneath Ibberton Hill the village is best reached from the A357 at Shillingstone.

Approx. distance of walk: 4⅓ miles. OS Map 194 ST 787/077.

There is a small car park behind the inn with limited space outside.

A most enjoyable scenic walk in this lovely peaceful area of rural Dorset, along tracks, field paths and quiet country lanes. After a hilly and demanding start the going gets easier having reached the village of Woolland.

Leave the inn and turn right, up the hill, past the church of St Eustaces and out into the lane at the top. Walk straight across, though the metal gate on the left to join the signed bridleway. Keep straight ahead beside the right-hand hedge and after passing under the power lines bear left up the hillside making for the small wooden gate in the far hillside. Fork right following the well trodden path down the hillside, along the gully bearing right at the bottom, across the track, and continue down to the brook.

Walk across and head up the track, past the farm dwellings and into the lane turning left and left again at the T junction uphill into Woolland. As an alternative there is signed footpath part way along the drive which will bring you out into the road just before reaching Woolland. The first mention of this little parish is a charter by King Althelstan, dated 939. As you walk past the church just look at the girth on the yew tree in the church yard.

Walk through the village and as you approach the bend keep straight ahead along the track signposted, to Stoke Wake. Go past the farm, and just before reaching the cottages pass through the gate into the field on the right and head straight across to the kissing gate in the far hedge. Keep close to

the hedge for a short distance then pass through the metal gate into the field on the right and go down to the stile in the far right-hand corner. Walk through the copse, over the stile in the fence and bear right across to the metal farm gate. Turn left at the farm, walking round the fence then through the metal gate into the farm entrance turning left up the drive and right into the lane.

Walk up to the T-junction at Woolland, turn right, and after passing two rows of cottages join the signed footpath on the left between the dwellings. Pass through the kissing gate and keep straight across the field, through the farm gate opposite and bear slightly right making for the stiles and crossing point in the opposite hedge. Cross the field to the far hedge walking round until you reach the stiles and plank bridge then cross into the field, over to another stile and maintain direction to the gate in the far corner.

Turn right onto the track and when you reach the thatched cottage take the grass path on the left leading to the stile, across to the stile in the hedge and finally over to the gate and down the lane back to the pub.

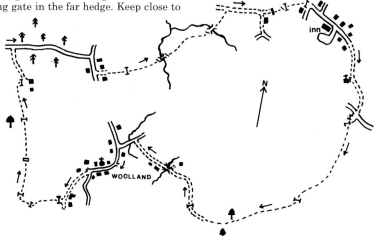

The Castle Inn, (West) Lulworth

Situated in one of the most beautiful and picturesque areas of Dorset is the lovely thatched Castle Inn. Originally designed by Inigo Jones it was built in the 17th century and known as 'The Jolly Sailor' but re-named after the castle that once existed nearby. Destroyed by fire in 1929 the inn has been painstakingly restored over the years. Today there are two main bars, the larger still retaining its original flagstone floor, a separate a la carte restaurant and a pleasant terrace in front of the inn, which is packed in summer with holiday makers and day-trippers visiting the cove. At the rear is a delightful illuminated, terraced garden and barbecue.

It is a Devenish house well run by the Halliday family. The bar is well stocked with a choice of three real ales.

Food is served both lunch times and evenings from 7 p.m. Apart from ploughman's, filled rolls, salads and jacket potatoes meals might include jugged hare with noodles, a curry, venison casserole or pigeon and bacon casserole. A wider choice of meals can be had in the flambe restaurant. Starters might include steamed shrimp with savoury sauce, peppered mushrooms or moules marinere followed by steak Diane, beef julienne, spicy lamb and yoghurt, scampi and crawfish provencale and carpet bag steak - the fillet stuffed with smoked oysters and mushrooms and served with a butter sauce - all flambe dishes are cooked at the table. Fish features strongly and could include a seafood stew of mussels, prawns, scallops and scampi or half a lobster stuffed with crab, spices and mushrooms, coated with cream and grilled with cheese.

Accommodation is available in 14 en-suite rooms ranging from singles to four poster beds.

In the summer the inn is open all day from 11 a.m. till 11 p.m., winter 10.30 a.m. till 2.30 p.m. and from 7 p.m. till 11 p.m.

Telephone: (01929) 400311

Situated on the B3070, the inn is on the right as you enter West Lulworth.

Approx. distance of walk: $3\frac{3}{4}$ miles. OS Map 194 SY 827/809.

Park in the inn's car park opposite or in the road at the front.

Dry underfoot this popular, scenic coastal walk, ideal for all the family, follows a country lane then descends across farm land to the coast before passing the famed Durdle Door and Lulworth Cove.

Turn right from the inn, down the hill and take the next turning right into West Street. Go past the church, up to the T-junction, cross the road and turn right. Walk to the top of the hill and turn left on the road signposted, to Durdle Door. Walk down towards the farm (ignoring the left turn into the caravan park). Bear right upon reaching the farmhouse then turn left onto the track following it up to the farm gate signposted, to Scratchy Bottom.

Walk down across the field to the gate in the bottom right-hand corner and follow the track ahead downhill, through a gate and up to a stile. Keep straight ahead skirting the field on the right and, upon reaching the stile, turn left onto the Dorset Coast Path. (if unfamiliar with the area it is advisable to keep well away from the cliff edge due to constant erosion.) Proceeding along this path you get a lovely view of Durdle Door.

Further on fork right following the sign to Lulworth Cove. Take time to enjoy the stunning scenery on your descent to the car park. Cross to the far side of the road and keep to the footpath uphill back to the pub. Whilst here it is worth a trip down the narrow traffic free street to the cove where there are a number of gift shops, cafes, restaurants and even another pub.

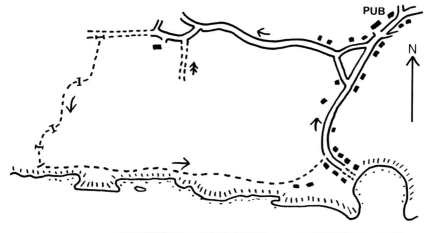

Durdle Door

The Angel Inn, Longham

Not that many years ago I can remember when The Angel had just small rooms for drinking whilst beer was kept in the rear kitchen. Over the years extensive alterations have taken place the last as recently as 1993 when a family area was added to the side. The work was skilfully carried out the pub loosing none of its character. Today the mostly open plan, beamed main bar is both comfortable, warm and welcoming. The bare brick and timber walls are decorated with a variety of stable, equine and other artefacts whilst the room is warmed in winter by an open log fire. There are several eating areas away from the bar, picnic benches at the front, with many more on the back patio together with a very good childrens' play area.

The inn is owned by Hall & Woodhouse and very well run by the long standing licensees Diane and Barry. The well stocked bar includes two real ales, Badger Best and Tanglefoot.

Served all week reliably good bar food includes traditional homemade steak and kidney pie, a roast beef platter, ham and fried egg and Spanish quiche some of which are available as smaller appetite meals. Sizzling skillets are available in the winter one of which is Szechuan chicken - julienne of chicken breast combined with a crisp Oriental vegetable mix and a hot chilli and tomato paste. The evening menu might list 'bang bang chicken' - cold breast fanned on a bed of lettuce coated with a peanut sauce followed by hake Portuguese - baked in a mushroom, tomato, onion and garlic sauce. Vegetarian specials such as mushroom and cranberry Wellington, broccoli and cream cheese bake and tuna and sweet corn bake are listed daily on the blackboard. Children have their own choice of meals.

Families welcome.

The inn is open all day from 11 a.m. till 11 p.m. (Sunday 12 noon till 10.30 p.m.) Telephone: (01202) 873778

Pub situated on the A348 between Poole and Ferndown.

Approx. distance of walk: $3\frac{1}{2}$ miles OS Map 195 SZ 068/991

In addition to the large car park at the side there is public lay-by just a short distance along the main road.

An interesting, easy going ramble through the Stour Valley on field paths, through woods and along the river bank.

Leave the pub carefully crossing the road into Angel Lane opposite. Follow this gravel bridleway, past the dwellings turning left at the cross track then next right towards Coneygar Farm. Just before reaching the farm entrance join the narrow signed footpath ahead, cross the stile and make for the gate on the left. Keeping close to the hedge walk up to the bridge, cross into the field and turn left along the well beaten path beside the ditch, through the trees and out into Ham Lane.

Carefully cross to the bridleway opposite signposted, Park Road $\frac{1}{2}$ mile. Ignore the track on the left but continue walking until you reach the stile then cross into the field on the left and turn left following the newly fenced path around the gravel workings. The path is well signed needing little explanation. Upon reaching the stile cross into the field on the right and make your way across to the far hedge bearing left to reach the stile. Turn left along the track then left again at the main road.

Just before reaching the thatched cottage cross over and join the river footpath sign-posted between the large house and the factory. Narrow at first it soon widens to a well maintained area of grass stretching between the golf course and the river bank. Many colourful dragonflies and butterflies can be seen in summer flying between teasels, purple loosestrife and yellow tansy. Cross the wooden bridge and climb the steep hill to reach the path at the top, turn left onto the tarred drive, walk up to the road and turn left.

Keeping to the wide grass verge cross over when you are opposite the footpath signposted, Heathlands Avenue following it up into the woods. A little care is now necessary to successfully negotiate your way through. First fork left following the well beaten path uphill through tall pines forking left again at the top. Disregarding the side paths keep straight ahead until you reach the point where the path rises over the bank ahead then bear left to pick up the path between the rhododendron bushes. Ignore the signed path on the left between two large oaks but continue ahead until you reach the clearing at which point turn left following the narrow path along the edge of the wood leading back into the woods. Fork left at the next path junction (waymarked) after which the path passes beside a field on the right before joining a track leading to the road at which point turn right back to the pub.

The Hambro Arms, Milton Abbas

The village of Milton Abbas originally stood on the land now occupied by the lake at the bottom of the hill but Joseph Damer, who rebuilt the abbey felt it spoilt his view and had the village razed and rebuilt in its present position. Today it is one of the most visited and photographed villages in Dorset if not the country.

Dating from around 1760 and altered over the years with a name change The Hambro Arms, in keeping with most of the buildings in this beautiful picture postcard village, is two-storey, thatched and wash painted white. A very atmospheric dining room with a large inglenook fireplace adjoins the main bar where an old world charm still pervades. Heated by a warm log fire in winter early prints and a collection of toby jugs decorate the walls of this comfortably furnished room. There is a separate public bar.

The inn has been well run for many years by the landlord Ken Baines maintaining the highest of standards. The bar is well stocked and includes two real ales Flowers Original and Boddingtons Bitter.

Particularly noted for its good food there are around fourteen daily blackboard specials such as liver and bacon, pork curry, fresh fish and local game. The printed menu which includes tasty homemade soup, Dorset pate, sandwiches and good sized ploughman's also lists salads and homemade quiche. My personal favourites are the lovely range of homemade pies such as steak and mushroom, game or beef and oyster served in their own individual dish and accompanied with a selection of really fresh vegetables.

There are two guest rooms, one twin bedded, the other with a four poster both rooms having en-suite facilities and a colour T.V.

Families are welcome in the dining room but no dogs.

Weekday opening times are from 11 a.m. till 2.30 p.m. and 6.30 p.m. till 11 p.m. Telephone: (01258) 880233

Village is best reached and signed from the A354 Blandford to Dorchester road at Winterborne Whitechurch.

Approx. distance of walk: $2\frac{1}{2}$ miles OS Map 194 ST 810/020.

Park at the front of the inn or in the road.

A short but delightful walk from this pretty prize winning village full of interest throughout which follows a route past the Abbey and beside the lake.

Turn right from the inn, go up the hill and join the signed footpath on the left climbing through the trees. Turn right into the cul-de-sac at the top, walk up to the road and turn right crossing over to join the narrow path up between the houses. Bear left across the playing fields, past the garages and turn right up the field past the new dwellings and through the gate. Follow the footpath beside the hedge all the way to the far side of the field, out onto the track and turn left.

Pass through the gate-house and keep straight ahead down the track through the woods. The last time I was here five deer suddenly crossed my path. Turn left at the bottom and keeping to the right-hand side of the road walk round until you reach the entrance to the abbey. Walk a short distance down and then left past the pay booth. (During school holidays only you may be asked to pay a small entrance fee to enter the grounds and visit the abbey)

Keep straight ahead through the grounds, past the school and famous Grass Staircase on the left which leads to a 12th century chapel. Just before reaching the tennis courts turn left onto the path beside the lake - home to many wildfowl. Enter the road on the far side, walk round the bend and turn left up through the village back to the pub.

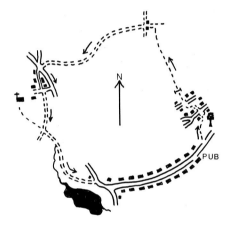

The Abbey

The Smugglers Inn, Osmington Mills

The Smugglers is a pretty thatched, stone-and-cob inn reputedly built in the 13th century. It was originally known as The Crown and was much associated with smuggling. The secret sign of the smugglers, which would indicate a safe house and friends willing to lend a hand, was the bottom of glass bottles cemented into the walls just below the eaves. The inn is in an idyllic spot nestling beside a stream only yards from the sea in this truly beautiful part of Dorset. The area has inspired many - not least Constable, who spent his honeymoon here; it was from this spot in fact that he painted his famous picture of Weymouth Bay. Popular with walkers following the Dorset Coast Path the inn has been added to over the years and now provides ample accommodation in the attractive interior with more seats on the front terrace.

The inn is a freehouse offering a good choice of drinks and real ales from the local Weymouth, Ringwood, Tisbury and Ruddles Breweries.

Despite a large number of people visiting the inn especially during the summer months food is served quickly and efficiently daily from midday till 2 p.m. and 7 p.m. till 9.30 p.m. Ordered from the servery two menus offer a choice of bar snacks such as tasty homemade soup, hot toasted baguettes, jacket potatoes and steak and kidney pie plus main meals like venison medallions lightly sauted and served with a rich blackcurrant and brandy sauce, chef's famous seafood and shell fish platter and 'Smugglers' seafood terrine served with a raspberry coulis. The Smugglers is well known for its lobster served grilled with garlic butter, cold with lemon mayonnaise or thermidor. There is a vegetarian menu presently offering a wild mushroom stroganoff and apple and Stilton bake, also meals for children and tempting puddings.

Weekday opening times are from 11 a.m. till 3 p.m. and 6 p.m. till 11 p.m (Sunday 12 noon till 3 p.m. and 6 p.m. till 10.30 p.m.)

The inn has 6 en-suite bedrooms.

Telephone: (01305) 833125

Osmington Mills is signposted at Osmington from the A353 between Weymouth and its junction with the A352, Dorchester to Wool road.

Approx. distance of walk: 3¼ miles OS Map 194 SY 735/817.

The inn has its own large car park on the hill opposite.

An easy going, scenic, very popular coastal walk (one of my favourites), suitable for all weather conditions which passes through Ringstead village and rises through a lush, almost tropical valley.

Walk to the back of the pub along the narrow inland path, climb the steps and stile and straight ahead to another, path is signed Ringstead 1. Little or no further explanation is necessary simply keep to the coastal path enjoying the views and maybe exploring one of the paths to the shore. At one point the path passes through an attractive lush valley before reaching Ringstead.

Turn left and walk up the approach road. During the summer there is a kiosk in the car park serving snacks and drinks. Continue up the hill round to the left then to the right turning left onto the gravel drive Go past the dwelling and fork right through the metal gate. Further on fork right again signposted, Upton 1½, walking until you reach the stile beside the gate. Climb over and turn right, over a crossing point and onto the well surfaced path which climbs gently through an attractive valley (lovely in the spring or summer when the wild flowers and unusual plants are at their best).

At the top cross the stile into the field, and keeping close to the hedge walk down to the stile at the bottom, and turn immediately left crossing the stile beside the gate signposted, to Osmington Mills. Follow the tarred road up to the stile along the track, over a second stile turning left upon reaching the tarred drive. Almost immediately take the signed path on the right, through the holiday park to the stile on the far side following the path ahead back to the pub.

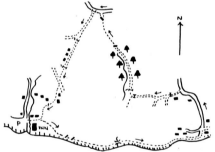

Looking towards Ringstead and White Nothe

The Thimble, Piddlehinton

One of my favourite Dorset inns, this very attractive, thatched pub nestles close to the river in the heart of the Piddle Valley. Originally two small bars the pub has been sympathetically enlarged using original materials. During construction a 22 feet well was discovered and is now an attractive feature in the hallway. The interior is comfortably furnished throughout and heated by an enclosed log fire set high in a brick fireplace.

The inn is a freehouse very well run by the friendly owners, Anne & Norman White and Susannah & Victor Lanfear. The bar is well stocked offering a good choice of real ales which include Ringwood's Old Thumper, cider and an excellent wine list which lists one first growth French claret.

Food is served all week from 12 noon till 2.30 p.m. and from 7 p.m. till 9 p.m. The extensive menu which includes specials like pigeon, beef and mushroom pudding and Cajun spiced lamb steak with grilled tomato also lists a tasty homemade soup, foie gras mousse with almonds and pears, fresh grilled mussels with garlic topped with cheese and sesame seeded chicken goujons with a honey and mustard dip followed by various grills, steak pie with traditional or red wine gravy, Guinness or Stilton gravy, grilled lamb chops with rosemary or simply Piddle Valley sausages with garnish and coleslaw, jacket potatoes, sandwiches and ploughman's. Vegetarians can choose between dishes like spinach & ricotta cannelloni verdi or a hot vegetable Balti. Sweets range from warm cherry pie with cream and treacle tart with custard to summer fruit pudding and toffee topolino - toffee ice cream on a meringue base with vanilla ice cream and praline pieces under a soft toffee sauce. Children have their own menu.

Families are welcome.

Opening times 12 noon till 2.30 p.m. and 7 p.m. till 11 p.m.

Telephone: (01300) 348270

Village is on the B3143 north of Dorchester.

Approx. distance of walk: 4 miles. OS Map 194 SY 713/975.

There is a good sized park at the rear of the pub plus parking lay-bys in the road.

A very enjoyable, scenic walk on well established paths and bridleways.

Leave the pub turning right and, after passing the lay-by turn right into the drive and join the raised stone footpath into the field, cross the bridge, make for the gate and turn left along the track, then right into the road. Walk a short distance up the hill until you reach a property on the left named, 'Honeypuddle'. Go up the drive, past the stables and through the gate in the corner keeping straight ahead to the gate on the far side, cross to a similar gate then bear left round to a wide farm gate. Pass through the second gate then bear right behind the buildings along the short track and through the gate on the right.

Keep to the track beside the hedge up the hillside and, upon reaching the gate go through into the adjoining field and turn right. Keep to the well marked grass track, through one gate and then another finally through a third and turn right following the limestone track downhill and up to the road.

Walk straight across onto the bridleway opposite, turn right at the cross track and bear left at the bend. After dipping to the valley the track rises to metal gates on top of the hill. Pass through the one on the right, keep straight ahead to a similar gate then down the track to the gate near the bottom. A lovely spot to view the valley.

Take the track on the right following it up to the gate and straight ahead, round the bend then pass through the metal gate into the field on the left. Cross the wooden bridge and either retrace your steps up to the stile and along the road back to the pub or follow the path across the field on the left (as the locals appear to do), crossing the stream and gap in the hedge into the rear car park of The Thimble.

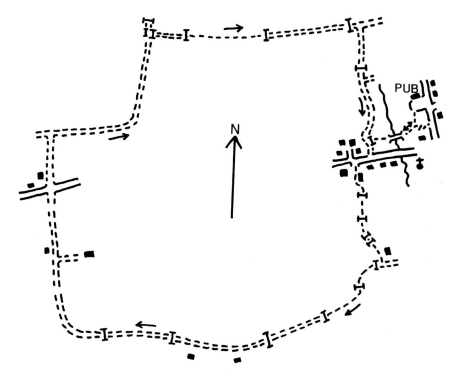

The Brace of Pheasants, Plush

The Brace of Pheasants must surely be one of the prettiest pubs in Dorset. Remotely situated in peaceful rural Dorset this 16th century thatched, brick and flint built inn was once two separate cottages and a forge and only became an inn in the mid 1930's. After a disastrous fire in 1979 it was re-built loosing none of its original charm. The cosy oak beamed main bar is heated by an open fire with a family room at one end and a very attractive restaurant the other. Outside there is a delightful rear beer garden with glorious views of the surrounding hills. It is a real family pub, very well run by its owners Jane and Geoffrey Knights. The well stocked bar can cater for all thirsts from country wines to draught cask conditioned cider plus three real ales.

Food at the "Brace" is excellent and served every day. Apart from tasty homemade soup and ploughman's the imaginative menu includes soft herring roes cooked with lemon and parsley butter, chicken liver and brandy pate served with a raspberry dressing, a warm salad of queens scallops and lardons of bacon tossed in garlic butter followed by breast of chicken served with a fresh orange and Grand Marnier sauce, tenderloin of pork with a grain mustard and basil sauce, steamed supreme of salmon with a lobster, tarragon and prawn sauce, fillet steak with a Port and Stilton sauce and game pie made with pigeon, pheasant and rabbit to name but a few. There is a vegetarian choice, a childrens' menu, a special three course lunch and daily specials which might include a goat's cheese in filo with a sweet pepper sauce also game in season.

Opening times are from 12 noon till 2 30 p.m. (Sun 3 p.m.) & 7 p.m. till 11 p.m. (Sun 10.30 p.m.)

Children welcome in the 'Old Kitchen'.

Telephone: (01300) 348357

From Dorchester take the B3143 to Piddletrenthide. Plush is signed to the right just beyond the village.

Approx. distance of walk: 4¼ miles. OS Map 194 ST 715/023.

Park beside the inn or in the surrounding lanes.

A very scenic and often bracing walk on farm land and established bridleways. Although hilly it is easy going with only the occasional muddy patch.

Leave the pub and take the Mappowder road opposite, walking round past the cottages and up the hill until you reach the signed footpath on the right. Pass through the metal gate and climb the sunken track to the stile then bear left across the field to the stile in the far hedge. Follow the beaten path ahead, past the concrete structure, through the gate into the field and turn left.

Keep close to the fence until you reach the signed bridleway on the left, go through the gate into the field and keep straight ahead along the ridge close to the boundary and trees on the right. Upon reaching the metal gate bear left and pick up the shallow track down the hillside to the gate. Pass through and keep straight ahead along the track, through the copse down past Folly Farm to the road. In springtime the area is abundant with garlic smelling ransoms, primroses and bluebells.

Walk straight across onto the signed bridleway opposite signposted, Alton Pancras. Very attractive and lined with ferns and wild flowers, this narrow track rises steadily to a gate. Pass through and keep straight ahead to a second then cross the field to the gate in the far right-hand corner. Follow the track through the trees, up to the gate and into the field.

Bear left and walk round keeping fairly close to the hedge on the right, and as you approach the far boundary arc to the left then go through the gap in the hedge on the left. Keep straight ahead gradually bearing left towards the metal gate uphill from the wood. Pass through onto the track, through a second gate and, after a pleasant descent to the road, turn left back to the pub.

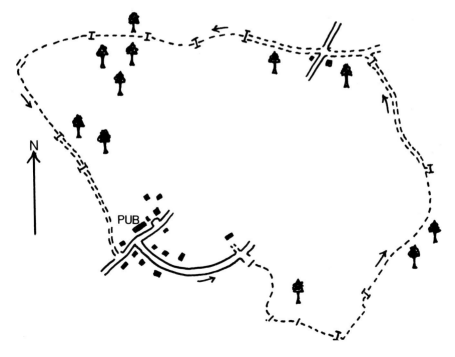

71

Three Horseshoes Inn, Powerstock

"The Shoes" as it is known locally is a Victorian inn built in 1906 after being destroyed by fire. Set in a large garden with fine views the main bar is comfortably furnished in the rustic manner whilst a separate dining room has wood panelled walls discovered after several layers of decoration were removed.

The inn is a Palmers house well run for a number of years by Pat and Diana Ferguson. The well stocked bar has a good range of wines plus three real ales.

Excellent food is available seven days a week based predominantly on fresh fish. Bought locally people travel from miles around to sample the lobster, skate, red mullet, john dory, squid and fresh mussels in season. Meat dishes include Dorset lamb and local game and for the less hungry a comprehensive snack menu is always on the go which includes at least two tasty homemade soups. To complete your meal there are tempting sweets like Dorset trifle and sticky toffee pudding.

The inn has four guest rooms - two en-suite.

Telephone: (01308) 485328. Fax: (01308) 485577

The pretty village of Powerstock, tucked peacefully away in the rolling hills of West Dorset is signed and best reached from the A356 Dorchester to Crewkerne road.

Approx. distance of walk: 3½ miles. OS Map 194 SY 517/961.

There is a car park beside the inn and space in the lane at the front.

A very scenic and pretty walk along peaceful country lanes, across farm land, beside the banks of a brook and through the small villages of South Poorton and West Milton. It can be challenging in places especially during wet weather when strong, waterproof footwear is recommended.

Leave the inn turning left, go past the church and head up the lane opposite, past a fine looking house and various attractive cottages forking right at the top of the village. Home to a variety of ferns including many heartstongues this shaded, high banked narrow lane rises steeply, flattens then dips steeply before rising again to the village of South Poorton. Turn left at the junction (a little path up the bank on the left cuts short the corner), walk past a tall barn and, just before reaching the dwelling take the signed footpath on the left. Uneven underfoot and sometimes running with water this attractive gully, shaded beneath a canopy of hazel trees, descends gradually towards the valley.

Near the bottom cross the stile beside the gate, enter the field and keep straight ahead until you eventually reach the stile in the hedge opposite. Enter the field turning left and, keeping close to the hedge, walk to the gate on the far side, go through and keep straight ahead following the well beaten path which dips beside the field boundary on the right to a pair of stiles in the corner. Maintain your direction across to the small gate and crossing point (just visible in the far hedge) through scrub and across an overgrown meadow to a stile.

Once more keep straight ahead following the path beside mature hazel trees, into another field and make for the gate opposite. In a few steps bear right, up and across the field to a stile beside a gate in the corner, through a gate and onto the bridleway. Turn left and pass through the farm gate into the lane at West Milton.

Turn left and almost immediately go left again up the grass path and steps to what remains of the late 15th century chapel of St Mary's. Walk to the gap in the back wall, over the crossing point into the field and straight ahead down to the gate and bridge opposite. Climb the narrow path then pass through the metal gate and follow the rather uneven and often muddy track before reaching a gate on the left. The path passes beneath a thick canopy of hazel trees then doglegs left up a rather bumpy incline before reaching one last gate. Turn right, walk up to the crossroads and right again back to the pub.

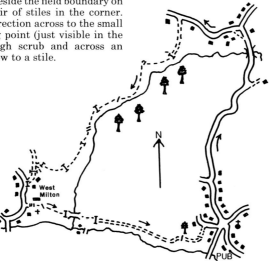

The Greyhound Inn, Sydling St. Nicholas

Entering the Sydling Valley one enters another world. The village, one of the prettiest and most peaceful in Dorset, was once known by the name "Aet Sidan Lalince" (at the broad hill) later Sidelyng and finally Sydling. St Nicholas is the saint to whom the village church is dedicated. Many old thatched, flint and brick cottages still exist. In 1859, when the population was 675, there were two bakers, one butcher, two grocers, one blacksmith, two cobblers, one tailor, one miller, two shopkeepers, two pubs and even a brewer. A few business still exist.

The Greyhound Inn which takes its name from the Sydling Greyhound, a strain of hunting dog bred in the area and featured in the crest of the Wyldbore Smith family is still today an important part of the village community. There is a generous bar area, conservatory, skittle alley and beer garden with a play area. The main bar has a part flag-stone floor and bare stone and flint walls. Separated by a large open brick fireplace is the attractive "Wishing Well" restaurant so named because of the twenty-two feet deep well with under water lighting. Upstairs a converted hay loft, the walls adorned with farming tools, serves as a function room seating up to fifty.

The inn is a freehouse well run by John and Sheena Parker. Five real ales are usually available including two regulars Eldridge Pope's Royal Oak and Hardy Country Bitter plus three guests one of which is often Tom Brown's Best Bitter from Goldfinch the Dorchester micro brewer.

Superb home-cooked food is available seven days a week in summer but not on Mondays during the winter months. Apart from snacks such as salads, plough-man's, homemade soup or chilli daily specials might range from fisherman's pie and chicken stroganoff to Sydling sizzler steaks. From the table d'hote restaurant menu you can choose a dish like avocado and walnut salad, venison in a green peppercorn sauce followed by strawberry brulee.

Weekday opening times are from 11 a.m. till 3 p.m. and 6 p.m. till 11 p.m.

Children are permitted in the restaurant areas, dogs too, under strict control. Telephone: (01300) 341303

The delightful village of Sydling St. Nicholas is signed from the A37 north of Dorchester at Grimstone.

Approx. distance of walk: 5 miles. OS Map 194 ST 633/996.

The pub has a car park at the front but alternatively you can park almost anywhere in the village.

A peaceful and very scenic easy going hill walk mostly on bridleways across open farm land.

Turn left from the pub walking down through the village then left again at the crossroads into East Street. After passing the green turn right onto the bridleway signposted, Large Bar Barn. At the end of the cul-de-sac keep straight ahead on the concrete farm road and take the gravel track on the left. When you reach the bend go through the gate ahead of you following the rough grass track, through a second gate and up the slope. Ignore the gate on the left but continue up through the gate into the field and straight across keeping close to the hedge on the left.

Cross the track at the top, pass through the gap in the hedge and continue ahead, down the field, through into the field ahead walking up until you reach the bridleway and turn right. Where the track bears to the right keep straight ahead into the field keeping to the rough grass track close to the hedge. At one point pass through a farm gate and continue ahead until you reach a small gate on the left, then go through and turn right onto a wide grass track. At the far

corner go through the gate and bear left across the field to meet the hedge on the left. Continue ahead, up to, and through a small gate and immediately turn right. Keeping close to the field boundary on the right walk down the meadow, through the farm gate, straight ahead through a similar gate and down to the track at the bottom. Turn right, go through a farm gate and bear left following the rough track, past the barn and walk round to the left keeping close to the wire fence, up to a gate and straight ahead on the track. Ignore the signed footpath on the left but continue ahead enjoying the lovely scenic view of the village. Bear right at the bottom, pass through the farm into the lane and turn right.

After about fifty yards cross the road and take the signed bridleway on the left. At the end of the narrow track turn right onto a wider track, pass through a couple of gates and go to the right of the farm buildings down to the lane. Turn left if you wish to visit the church otherwise continue straight ahead on the bridleway signposted, Break Heart Hill. A short distance along the track look for a stile in the hedge on the right, go over, across the field to the stile opposite and follow the narrow path behind the houses, out into the lane and turn left back to the pub.

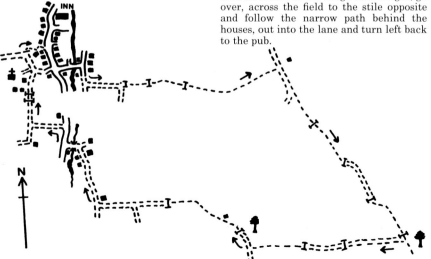

The Anchor Inn, Seatown

The Anchor is a very popular inn especially with walkers following the Dorset Coast Path being sited almost on the beach in the delightful village of Seatown. Inside there are two small cosy bars, adorned with various photographs and nautical regalia plus a separate family room. Picnic benches are neatly positioned to make the most of the sunny front terrace whilst enjoying the bracing sea air and the view of the spectacular Dorset coast line.

The inn is owned by Palmers, the local Bridport brewery and very well and efficiently run for the past 12 years by Dave and Sadie Miles. In addition to a warming cup of hot chocolate four real ales regularly available are Bridport Bitter, the stronger Tally Ho, I.P.A. and Palmers 200.

Food is served every day of the week with imaginative specials such as prawn jambalaya with melon, seafood casserole and avocado and crab salad served hot with grilled cheese. In addition to the usual pub snacks like tasty homemade soup, ploughman's, jacket potatoes, sandwiches and pizzas there are various homemade pies, hot 'n' spicy chicken, a selection of grills and usually a tasty curry. Being a coastal pub sea food naturally features strongly with crab, prawn and lobster salads and a seafood platter in the evening consisting of mussels, prawns, cockles, crab-meat and smoked mackerel. Popular with pudding lovers is the homemade apple pie served with clotted cream. There is a separate childrens' menu.

Families welcome.

From Whitsun through till September the inn is open all day from 11 a.m. till 11 p.m. with teas served between 3 p.m. and 5 p.m.. Winter hours 11 a.m. till 2.30 p.m. and 7 p.m. till 11 p.m.

For anyone wishing to stay overnight there are two comfortable rooms overlooking the beach having T.V., radio, kettle, toaster and fridge - continental breakfast is taken in the room by the window.

Telephone: (01297) 489215

Seatown is signposted from the A35 at Chideock. Follow the narrow lane down to the beach.

Approx. distance of walk: 3½ miles. OS Map 193 SY 420/918.

Park in the road at the front or the large car park opposite.

Golden Cap at 617 feet is the highest cliff on the south coast and the path to the top is probably the most popular in Dorset; it is certainly the most scenic. Although some sections are quite steep the walk is not over demanding.

From the inn walk back up the lane, past the telephone kiosk and round to the left. After passing the farm-house go over the stile on the left following the path up and round to a crossing point. Cross the field on the well trodden path up to a crossing point on the far left side. Go over the bridge, up the path to another crossing point, across the field to the gate and up the embankment onto the Dorset Coast Path.

Turn right climbing up the hill towards the crossing point, go into the field and bear right making your way up towards Langdon Hill and the crossing point in the top right-hand corner. Turn left following the path up to a wooden gate, pass through into the field and go left up towards another crossing point at which point turn right following the sign to St Gabriel's. Walk round the field for a short distance until you reach a farm gate on the left (bridleway signposted) pass through and cross the field to the far side.

From here you can short cut across the field and join the path leading directly to Golden Cap but to complete the walk keep to the track down to the bottom left-hand of the field past the remains of St. Gabriels Church, a good spot to stop for awhile. Turn left and walk back up the hill to the crossing point and climb steeply to the summit.

After taking in the view follow the path round, past the trig. point and down the far side to a crossing point after which turn right following the Dorset Coast Path down-hill back to Seatown. Just before reaching the bottom take the path off to the right, down the steps to the beach and back to the inn.

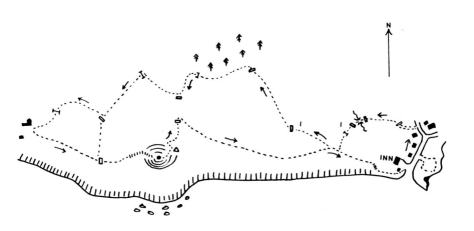

The Cricketers, Shroton (Iwerne Courtney)

Overlooking the green beneath Hambledon Hill this friendly village pub, originally thatched, dates from the 1800's but was rebuilt by the Victorians after a disastrous fire. The mainly open plan bar has two seating areas, a games section and non-smoking area with lots of cricket regalia displayed on the walls. There is also a restaurant seating up to 30 and an attractive beer garden.

The inn is a free house very well run by the owners Bobby and Sarah Pillow. There are three constantly changing real ales chosen from a list of at least 20 beers such as Ringwood Brewery's Fortyniner, Smiles Bitter and Bass.

Since taking over the pub in 1989 the owners have built up a very good food trade warranting inclusion in several good food guides. Served all week you can choose from freshly prepared bar snacks like homemade soup, ploughman's and baguettes with various fillings or pick one of the many blackboard specials. Heading the list on my last visit was homemade steak and Guinness pie, prawns wrapped in filo pastry served with garlic mayonnaise, salad and hash browns. Day boat catches include Dover sole, red mullet with a cream, dill and Dijon sauce and other imported tropical fish. The more comprehensive restaurant menu offers starters ranging from deep fried cheese with apricot and Drambuie sauce to oven baked mushrooms stuffed with Stilton cheese and coated with bread crumbs. Main course meals include chicken breast with a Stilton and walnut sauce, poached salmon with herb butter and oatmeal chive pancakes filled with spinach and cream cheese on a tomato and herb sauce. A traditional roast is served Sunday lunchtimes together with a small a la carte menu. There is always a selection of homemade sweets.

Children are welcome and dogs too if kept on a lead but muddy boots are definitely not.

Opening times can be flexible but usually from 11.30 a.m. till 2.30 p.m. and 7 p.m. till 11 p.m.

Telephone: (01258) 860421

Village is signed from the A350 4 miles north of Blandford

Approx. distance of walk: 2½ miles. OS Map 194 ST 859/127.

Although the inn has its own car park you can leave your car almost anywhere in the road or by the green.

A very scenic walk for that sunny Sunday which takes you high up onto Hambledon Hill. Although fairly strenuous there are no stiles and the going is mostly good underfoot. For a longer walk you can combine this one with the walk from Childe Okeford on page 20 picking it up at the trig. point.

Turn right from the pub, through the village turning right again when you reach the Childe Okeford road. Continue up and round the bend to pick up the signed bridleway on the left. Bearing left walk up the hill and onto the track. Pass through the gate then turn right, through one more gate to join the track up the hillside taking time as you go to look over your shoulder and enjoy the magnificent view over the village and north to Iwerne Minster.

Keep climbing until you reach the trig. point at the top and unless combining this walk with that from Childe Okeford, turn left walking down the field beside the boundary. At the bottom turn right onto the signed bridleway then pass through the gate into the field keeping straight ahead close to the left-hand boundary.

Pass through the gate and continue following the track down through another gate and past the barn walking until you reach a small gate on the left. Go through following the narrow path up to a further gate and into the field. Keep straight ahead up the rise, pass through the gate re-tracing your steps down the field to the gate at the bottom. Enter the lane turning left, and in fifty paces take a small path on the right leading straight into the back garden of the pub.

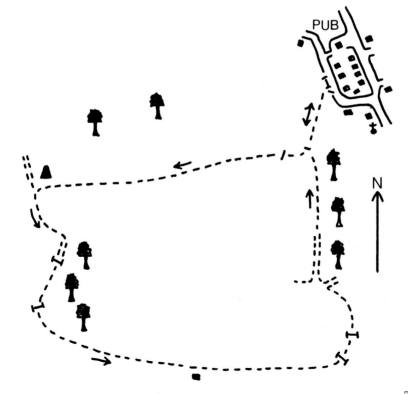

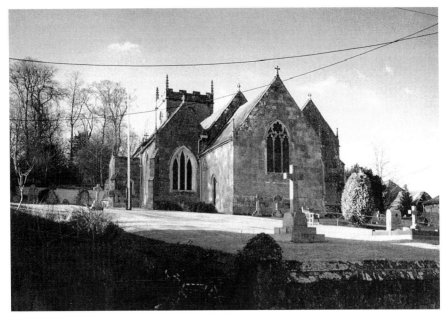

The church of St. Mary, Shroton

Old Harry Rocks

The Bankes Arms, Studland

Built from local Purbeck stone and occupying an enviable position overlooking Studland Bay, The Bankes Arms is both an hotel and an inn. In 1990 the interior was completely re-furbished combining the rear bar and family room the work carried out sympathetically using matching stone. There is an open fire in winter. In summer there are tables at the front but the most sought after are those in the field opposite with lovely views across the bay.

Owned by The National Trust the inn is well run by the friendly licensees, Mrs & Mrs Lightbrown. Up to six constantly changing real ales are the norm here with beers such as Castle Eden, Royal Wessex, Smiles Bitter and locally brewed Poole Best Bitter. If you need warming after your walk the landlord is presently building a good selection of single malts.

Food is available at lunch times, every evening, all day during the summer and Saturday and Sunday in the winter. Apart from the usual snacks like ploughman's the blackboard menu over the fireplace lists several fish specialities which might include prawns in garlic, fresh crab salads in season, local red and grey mullet and sea bass, caught by his son, which is baked in foil with herbs. Cream teas are served daily in the summer between 3.30 and 5.30 p.m

Families welcome, dogs on a lead.

From Whitsun until mid-September opening times are from 10.30 a.m. till 11 p.m. (Sunday 10.30).

The inn has nine letting rooms, one a single, most with en-suite bathrooms but all with T.V. and tea making facilities.

For those arriving by boat the inn has four moorings in the bay.

Telephone: (01929) 450225. Fax: (01929) 450307

Walk No. 34

Studland can be reached either from Sandbanks using the car ferry or by taking the A351 from Wareham to Corfe and then the B3351. The inn is on the right on the road leading to the beach.

Approx. distance of walk: 3¾ miles OS Map 195 SZ 037/825.

Although there is only limited road parking at the pub the National Trust own a large car park close by but do levy a charge in summer.

Good underfoot this often bracing but very scenic coastal walk crosses Ballard Down and rounds Old Harry and Handfast Point passing through a small wooded area filled with garlic smelling ransoms.

From the car park go behind the inn to a stile set in the fence on the left, cross the field to the stile opposite and turn right into the road. Continue walking for a short distance turning left at the War Memorial to join the bridleway signposted, Swanage 1¾ miles. Walk uphill, past several dwellings and where the track bears right pass through the gate on the left following the track up onto Ballard Down.

At the top pass through the gate and turn left along the Swanage Coastal Path taking time as you go to admire the magnificent panoramic views. Continue along this path, through another gate following the sign for Old Harry Rocks. Keep walking until you reach the trig. point then take the centre path which leads down to Handfast Point and the rocks. From here simply follow the path around the point, through the small wood the air of which is filled with the smell of garlic in springtime and back to Studland forking right by the blackthorn hedge. Turn right into the road back up the hill to the pub.

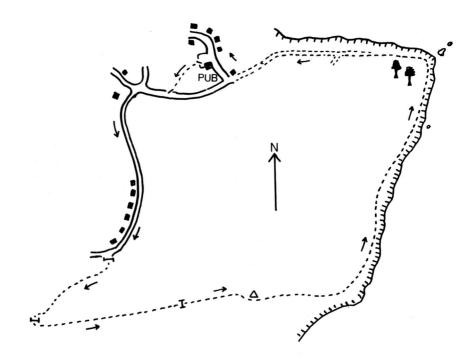

The New Inn, Stoke Abbott

The New Inn at Stoke Abbott is a part thatched, brick and stone building dating from the 17th-century and became an inn in the middle of the 1800's; prior to that it was known as Stocks Farm. Today it is the centre of village life, well run by the friendly licensees. Comfortably furnished with spindleback chairs and wooden settles the cosy beamed main bar has a thatched canopy over the servery and a large collection of horse brasses. A large inglenook fireplace dominates the end wall. There is a separate dining room/family room and a nice lawned beer garden at the back.

The inn is a Palmer's House with a well stocked bar which includes a choice of wine plus three real ales Bridport Bitter, Palmers's IPA and 200.

Food is available every day from 12 noon till 2 p.m. and 7.30 p.m. till 9.00 p.m. (No food Sunday evening). Supplemented by daily blackboard specials like grilled mullet, sea bass fillets, fresh local crab, lagostinos, breast of pheasant, curry and lemon chicken cooked in coriander, ginger and garlic the menu lists the Stoke Abbott platter of English cheeses - Stilton, mature Cheddar, Somerset Brie and Shropshire blue. There is also tasty soup, baguettes, jacket potatoes and freshly made salads. Main dishes include homemade chicken and ham pie, various grills, fried scampi wholetail plus a childrens' menu and three vegetarian dishes which include leek and Roquefort tart, Brie, potato and courgette almond crumble and wild mushroom strudel with brandy sauce.

Weekday opening times are from 12 noon till 3.00 p.m. and 7 p.m. till 11 p.m. (Sunday 10.30 p.m.)

Families are welcome but no dogs.

The inn has three letting rooms - one twin and two doubles.

Telephone: (01308) 868333

Walk No. 35

From the centre of Bridport take the B3162 Broadwindsor road. Stoke Abbott is signed 3½ miles north. The pub is at the end of the village on the right.

Approx. distance of walk: 4 miles OS Map 193 SY 455/007.

In addition to the rear car park there is some limited space in the road at the front.

Stoke Abbott is a pretty peaceful Dorset village where time appears to have stood still. The walk, very scenic, hilly, occasionally muddy and demanding in places explores field paths, an old drove track, country lanes and woods and enters the small village of Netherbury.

Turn left from the pub uphill through the village, past the church keeping straight ahead at the bend, and a short way along the gravel track pass through the gate into the field on the right. Cross to the gap in the far hedge and walk to the stile opposite by the thatched cottage, climb down the steps to the drive, turn right and almost immediately cross the stile into the field on the left bearing right down to the bridge.

Cross into the field, walk up to the hedge and turn left, pass through the metal gate and go down the field making for the dwellings at the bottom. Pass between the buildings, through the metal gate and bearing right follow the sunken track up the hillside, through a gate and up onto the ridge. Pass through the gate on the right and turn left along the track.

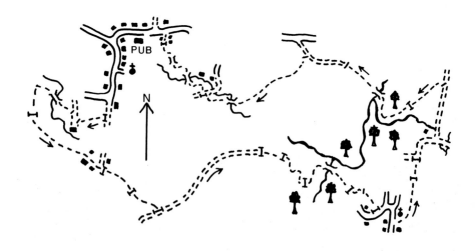

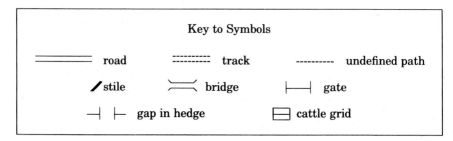

Key to Symbols

road   track   undefined path

stile   bridge   gate

gap in hedge   cattle grid

84

Keep straight ahead along the main track (muddy at times) and after a long walk pass through the gate into the field and walk down making for the metal gate in the furthermost point. Go down the bank, cross the stream and up to the gap at the top, into the field and turn left. Walk round beside the hedge, through the small wooden gate following the attractive woodland path down to the stream, over the plank bridge and up the steep field path to the small gate at the top. Bear left to the stile and walk down the field beside the hedge and through the gate into the road.

Keep straight ahead down the hill and after passing the church turn left by the War Memorial and join the footpath signposted, to Beaminster. This attractive narrow path passes round the church and leads to a kissing gate. Follow the beaten path ahead down to the gate and along the track turning right at the bottom then left up the drive. Upon reaching the stile cross into the field on the left, then bear left down across the field to the small gate in the far hedge, walk down to the wooden bridge but do not cross instead turn right and follow the path around the bank until reaching a similar bridge. Cross into the field and bear left up to the gate and along the track.

Either walk to the lane and turn left back to the pub or more enjoyably join part of the recently signed Jubilee Trail created by the Ramblers Association in 1995. Before reaching the road cross a series of stiles on the left, well waymarked then down across the hillside, through a gap in the thicket down to the bridge and up to the stile on the right. Cross the track onto the very attractive path opposite which almost immediately bears left up through the trees. On the far side of the wood cross the bridge into the field, walk up to the bridge on the right then follow the path up the bank, through the gates, up to the road and turn left back to the pub.

Stoke Abbott

The Ilchester Arms, Symondsbury

Symondsbury is an attractive village on the outskirts of Dorchester, almost every house is pleasing to the eye including the 18th century rectory and the 16th century Ilchester Arms - a two-storey thatched inn built from local stone and extended over the years. The cosy main bar has a large open fire whilst candles top the tables in the other used mainly for dining in the evening and at weekends. The inn also has a skittle alley and streamside beer garden.

It is a Palmers house well run by the licensees Dick and Ann Foad. The well stocked bar includes a good selection of wines and three real ales, Bridport Bitter, Palmers Traditional Best Bitter and either Tally Ho or Palmers 200.

The inn has always had a reputation for excellent food a standard maintained by the present licensees. There are various menus wherever you eat. The printed menu lists various starters and cold snacks including their speciality garlic baguette and prawns also 'Hikers' rolls, 'Ramblers' jacket potatoes and 'Walkers' ploughman's. There are fish dishes, beef in beer, homemade cottage pie and a lamb cassoulet whilst the constantly changing chalkboard might list smoked salmon pate, homemade soup, avocado and sweet herring and a smoked haddock crepe followed by chicken breast chausser, homemade chicken and vegetable pie and a vegetarian mixed bean casserole. The inn offers a separate childrens' menu and a reasonably priced Sunday lunch. Sweets range from whisky and mince tart and treacle roly-poly to cold boozy trifle and toffee topolino.

Children of all ages are welcome in all areas of the pub and skittle alley and there is no objection to dogs.

Weekday opening times are fairly flexible depending upon the season but the inn is usually open from 11.30 a.m. till 3 p.m. and 6.30 p.m. till 11 p.m.

Overnight accommodation is available.

Telephone: (01308) 422600

Symondsbury is signposted west of Bridport from the A35. The inn is in the centre of the village close to the church.

Approx. distance of walk: 4¾ miles. OS Map 193 SY 444/936.

Park in the road at the front or in the rear car park.

Symondsbury is typical of the many pretty, unspoilt ham stone villages in this lovely area of Dorset. The walk is very scenic along field paths, wide gravel tracks and attractive sunken gullies festooned with wild flowers and ferns

Leave the pub turning right then next right on the Broad Oak road, past the church and straight ahead down the hill. As you approach the bend join the signed footpath on the right. Walk a few steps up the drive, go right across the bridge and left up to the stile. Walk across the field, over the stile and over to a pair of stiles either side of the drive. Bear right across to the bridge, cross into the field and leave by the gate. Turn left and almost immediately go through the gate into the field on the right. Bearing left walk up to the far hedge walking along until you reach the chain link squeeze stile. Follow the attractive path ahead up thorough the thicket, then left round the hillside and down to the gate. Turn right along the sunken track and upon reaching the road join the signed footpath on the left beside the entrance to the Community Hospital.

Walk up this very attractive fern lined gully, keeping straight ahead at the top between the fields finally crossing the stile into the field. Keep straight ahead, through the gate then walk round the field to the left until you reach a wide metal gate. Go into the field and bear left across to the stile, walk down the grass path behind the dwelling then cross the stile into the field on the left and walk down to the bridge at the bottom. Go up the field bearing right and when you reach the metal gate pass through onto the wide grass area. Walk up keeping to the left of the woods, then along the track and up to the road.

Cross into the drive of Axen Farm following this track for some distance, past the dwelling and farm buildings, through the gate, uphill to the track and turn left. There are good views over Chideock and to the sea beyond. Go past the barn and straight ahead down the track, forking left further ahead and gently descend this very attractive fern lined drove road. In places the gully is deeply cut with high sand stone cliffs. After a long descent the track leads directly back to the pub.

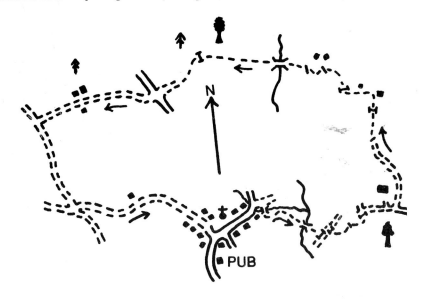

The Langton Arms, Tarrant Monkton

This very attractive 17th-century thatched pub can be found next to the church in the sleepy picturesque village of Tarrant Monkton. Inside there are two bars, one wonderfully atmospheric with a large open fireplace, the other more comfortable and mainly for dining, has circular bench seating, window seats and heated by a warm wood burning stove. There is a separate restaurant, skittle alley and family room also a large beer garden with childrens' play area.

The inn is a freehouse well run by the licensees Barbara and James Cossins. The well stocked bar presently includes four real ales from a constantly changing list such as Morland Old Speckled Hen, Shepherd Neame Spitfire, Smiles Best Bitter, Ringwood Fortyniner and 1066 from The Hampshire Brewery.

Food is served in the bar everyday from 12 noon till 3 p.m. and 6 p.m. till 10 p.m. (Sunday 6.30 till 9.30). A sample selection of blackboard specials might include a tasty soup like Stilton and celery, local roast partridge in a claret sauce, liver and bacon in a red wine and onion gravy, supreme of chicken in a lemon and bacon sauce, wild boar and apple sausages and Somerset Brie wrapped in filo pastry with cranberry sauce. Vegetarians have a good choice which includes mushrooms in cream topped with a pastry lid and pasta parcels filled with spinach and ricotta in a tomato and basil sauce. Meals on the menu in the restaurant (open Wednesday - Saturday evenings and Sunday lunch times) include warm salad of baby scallops finished with parsley butter and a ragout of forest mushrooms with brandy and cream followed by roast rack of minted lamb and sauteed English calves liver with oyster mushrooms in a rich Madeira sauce.

Weekday opening times are from 11.30 a.m. till 3 p.m. and 6 p.m. till 11 p.m, all day Saturday 11.30 a.m. till 11 p.m. and Sunday from 12 noon till 10.30 p.m.

Children are welcome in the family room and there is no objection to dogs in the pub.

The inn has overnight accommodation in six double rooms.

Tel: (01258) 830255. Fax: (01258) 830053

Tarrant Monkton is signed from the A350 Wimborne to Blandford road at Tarrant Keyneston.

Approx. distance of walk: 4 miles. OS Map 195 ST 944/088.

Park at the front or rear of the inn or in the road by the war memorial.

A very enjoyable, scenic walk along well surfaced drove tracks and field paths perfect for a sunny day.

Leave the pub turning left, go past the war memorial and cross The Tarrant. Keep straight ahead past the thatched cottages forking left at the bend into Turners Lane. This tarred and gravel track rises steadily between high hedged fields before meeting a cross track at which point turn right.

Follow this very scenic drove track (a good place to pick sloes) for about a mile turning right at the cross track (lovely views over the Tarrant Valley). Keep walking beside woods on the left turning left at the next cross track then fork right through Hogstock, past the cottages and right at the road junction.

Keeping to the grass verge on the right walk round and down Hogstock Hill turning right at the bottom. Keep to the right-hand side of the road carefully crossing over when you reach the entrance to Luton

Farm. Walk down this tarred farm road again crossing The Tarrant then bear left past the farm buildings, up through two farm gates onto the track beyond and almost immediately pass through the gate into the field on the right.

Keeping close to the buildings walk straight across to the stiles in the corner then bear left up to the stile in the far hedge. Maintain your direction across this field, over another stile and up the rise making for the gate in the corner. Turn right along the farm road, past the buildings until you reach farm gates on the left. Pass through in to the field and, bearing right walk down to the gate in the far corner, enter the field ahead walking until you reach the stile, go into the adjoining field and follow the well beaten path down to the stile leading directly into the car park of the pub.

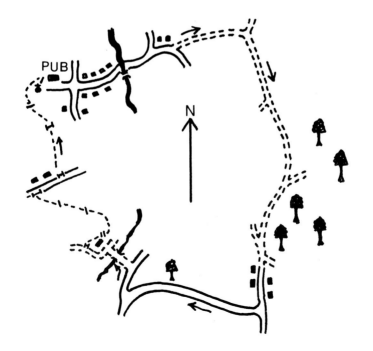

The Wise Man, West Stafford

This quaint thatched, 400 year old inn is tucked on the outskirts of Dorchester in the small village of West Stafford. Thomas Hardy used the village church of St. Andrew as the scene of Tess's marriage to Angel Clare. Accommodation comprises two bars, a comfortable cosy lounge bar and a simply furnished but homely public bar heated by a warm open fire and which features a collection of Toby jugs and cases of antique pipes collected from around the world by a previous landlord. Adding a touch of colour, Morris men can sometimes be seen in the summer dancing on the forecourt, the sight of which can be enjoyed sitting at the tables in front of the pub. The contained rear beer garden offers further seating for up to 32 people in very pleasant surroundings.

David Bailey, the newly appointed landlord of this Greenhalls pub, is a real ale enthusiast who serves two regular real ales, Draught Bass and Marston's Pedigree plus two guest ales such as Ringwood Old Thumper and Old Speckled Hen.

Food is served all week except Sunday evenings in the winter. Apart from snacks like homemade soup, sandwiches and ploughman's with interesting local cheeses, typical blackboard specials might include a homemade turkey curry, homemade beef chassuer, steak and ale pie, pork escallope - pan fried with a white wine, mushroom and garlic sauce, game in season, fresh cod cooked in the pub's own beer batter and for vegetarians a vegetable lasagne or broccoli and cream cheese bake. For the sweet toothed there are sorbets and traditional English puds like spotted dick, jam roly poly and lemon sponge. There is a roast on Sunday.

Families and dogs are equally welcome.

Weekday opening times are from 11 a.m. till 3 p.m. and 6 p.m. till 11 p.m.

Telephone: (01305) 263694

West Stafford is signed from the Dorchester by-pass alternatively turn of the A35 Troy Town by-pass and take the turning signposted, to Higher & Lower Bockhampton. Keep straight ahead at the crossroads, through lower Bockhampton and turn left at the road junction.

Approx. distance of walk: 5½ miles. OS Map 194 SY 726/896.

Park at the front or in the side car park.

Quite long and a little demanding this very enjoyable and interesting walk is both historical and scenic taking in the birthplace of Thomas Hardy, the area where he grew up and Stinsford Church where he worshipped, and where his family, together with his own heart, are now buried. Generally good underfoot the walk crosses open heath and farm land, passes through attractive woods and along peaceful country lanes and tracks; it both crosses and follows the banks of the River Frome and its tributaries, and passes through the tiny villages of Higher and Lower Bockhampton.

Leave the inn and follow the lane up and out of the village to the left. You will soon see the Manor House on your left. After passing a sign which reads "concealed entrance 100 yards" turn left into the Dairy House drive and immediately go through the metal gate into the field on the right and across the field bearing left down to the crossing point in the far hedge. Walk to the stile opposite, across the next field and over the stile onto the narrow path which bears right into the lane.

Turn left along the track, pass through the gate, cross both bridges and go through the gate ahead of you into the field. Follow the path ahead, over the plank bridge then cross the stile into the field and turn right. In fifty paces negotiate the wooden bridge over the river and make for the metal gate opposite. Keep to the wide grass track (muddy in places), leave by the far gate and turn left. Keep to the signed bridleway, cross the concrete bridge and almost immediately pass through the gate into the field on the left. Keeping close to the hedge walk round and up the field to the gate then follow the track ahead round the farm buildings and out into the road.

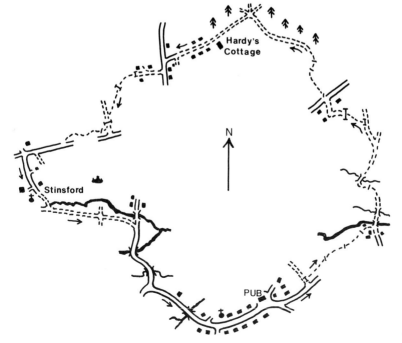

Walk straight across to the stile opposite, enter the field and keep straight ahead making for the stile in the far boundary, over a second stile and then bear right onto the wide path which rises at first, dips and then heads very steeply up Durdle Heath. Bear left at the top and keep walking along this wide track for quite some distance until you eventually reach the junction of five at which point turn left. Bat boxes can be seen attached to the surrounding trees. Keep to this track which will eventually lead you to Hardy's Cottage.

The exterior is open from the 1st April until 30th October daily, except Thursday, from 11 a.m. till 5 p.m. Interior by appointment only. Continue past the cottage along the gravel road, up to the lane and turn left. Soon join the bridleway on the right signposted, Kingston Maurward 1 Stinsford 1¼. Walk down to the barn at the end of the gravel track, pass through the small metal gate walking down the field to the gate at the bottom. Follow the diversion (if in place) otherwise bear left across the field to the gate on the far side, pass through, cross to the stile on the right and take the narrow path uphill through the woodland strip and out through the gate into the road at the top.

Turn right, go past the entrance to Kingston Maurward College and take the next left signposted, Stinsford Church. The graves of the Hardy family are on the left as you enter the churchyard. Leave by the rear gate into the lane and follow the attractive bridleway ahead turning left towards Lower Bockhampton. This very attractive path runs beside the stream from which you have a good view of Kingston Maurward House. Upon reaching the lane turn right then left at the road junction and, keeping to the right-hand side carefully walk the half mile back to West Stafford.

The birthplace of Thomas Hardy

The Lamb Inn, Winkton

The Lamb Inn at Winkton (or to be more precise, using the old Parish name, Holfleet) is the most easterly inn in this book occupying an idyllic spot surrounded by fields. The main lounge is comfortably and tastefully furnished in an old world charm with a beamed ceiling. There is a separate restaurant/function room and a cosy public bar overlooking fields at the front. Heated by an open log fire the room has a sensibly placed dartboard, piano and a stuffed fish in a case on the wall together with horse brasses etc. Fine weather drinkers may care to sit on the sunny front terrace or in the beer garden where there is a childrens' play area.

The well stocked bar presently includes two beers from the Ringwood Brewery - their Best and Fortyniner also two from the Hampshire Brewery - King Alfred's and Edmond Ironside a well balanced traditional bitter.

Food is served all week from 12 noon till 2 p.m. and from 6.30 p.m. till 9.30 p.m. Pub snacks include soup of the day, various ploughman's such as cowman's with roast beef and cheese and fisherman's with smoked mackerel. Also baked potatoes with various fillings, sandwiches and omelettes. More substantial meals listed on the menu are homemade dishes of steak & kidney pie in brown ale, chilli, chicken chasseur, a curry and salads with home-cooked ham or beef. Vegetarian dishes include a country cheese bake whilst children have a choice of three meals. Food specials might include a grilled halibut steak, local pan fried trout or the house speciality 'smothered steak' a pan fried minute steak topped with fried onions and mushrooms, coated with cheese and grilled.

Opening times, Monday till Friday are from 11 a.m. till 3 p.m. and 5.15 p.m. till 11 p.m. Saturday 11 a.m. till 11 p.m. and Sunday 12 noon till 3 p.m. and 7 p.m. till 10.30 p.m.

Families are welcome, dogs too both inside and in the garden if under control. Telephone: (01425) 672427

Walk No. 39

From the B3347, Ringwood to Christchurch road turn left in to Burley Road at Winkton (just past The Fisherman's Haunt). The pub is on the right at the end of the village.

Approx. distance of walk: 2½ miles. OS Map 195 SZ 166/963.

There is an ample car park at the pub plus parking space in the road at the back.

A short but pleasant, mostly level walk on field paths, green roads and peaceful country lanes. Best walked in the summer it is ideal for all the family especially as there are many farm animals to be seen on-route.

From the pub turn left into Burley Road, walk to the end of the pavement and cross to the opposite verge. In about eighty paces join the signed public footpath on the right climbing the bank to the stile and head across the field to the stile in the wire fence. Maintain direction to the far stile, go out into the lane and turn left. (Alternatively you can turn right into Burley Road and then next left into the lane). Turn right when you reach the signed footpath following this wide grassy track round to the right and out into the lane.

Turning left cross over to the wide grass verge along the road past the farm and several dwellings before reaching a track on the right. Follow this green road between the fields, out into the Bockhampton road and straight across into Hawthorn Road. Keep to this peaceful lane and just before reaching the dwelling enter the field on the right, footpath signposted. Walk straight ahead to the far side and cross the lane into the field ahead. Maintain your direction to the far side, through a gap in the hedge keeping to the hedge on the right. At the end of the field turn right along the narrow tree lined grass track until you reach the road then turn left over the bridge back to the pub.

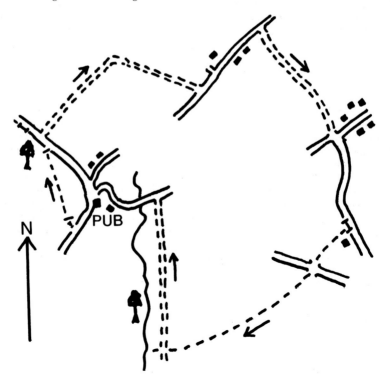

The Square & Compass, Worth Matravers

The lovely unspoilt Square & Compass, situated in a high spot above the picturesque village of Worth Matravers, is a welcome sight after the long haul up from the cliff's edge. Built in the 17th century from local stone and painted white it is without doubt the most original pub still left in Dorset. The Square & Compass, depicted on the inn sign, are a stonemason's basic tools and honours the men who cut the marble from the nearby quarries. Today it is still a symbol used by Freemasons. A narrow stone passageway leads to a small servery where the beer is kept. To the left is the Tap Room, small and cosy with a wood burning stove whilst the lounge on the other side of the passage has a low ceiling, stone fireplace and wood block floor. Assorted furnishings consist of a piano and an old record player together with a large collection of 78 discs. Assorted paraphernalia littered around include Charlie's own collection of local fossils. There is a small rear beer garden but my preference is to sit on one of the rustic seats on the sunny front terrace looking out to sea whilst chickens scratch about my feet.

The inn is now a freehouse, thankfully Charlie bought the freehold from Whitbread in 1994. He took over the licence from his father Ray in 1993 who in his turn managed the pub after his grandfather. Beers kept are mostly from Whitbread such as Strong Country plus Ringwood Fortyniner and Hall & Woodhouse Tanglefoot all still served traditionally straight from the barrel. Also stocked is Bulmers Traditional cider and Murphy's stout.

Although food is very limited freshly cooked pasties are always available.

Families and dogs welcome.

The inn is open daily from 11.30 a.m. till 3 p.m., 6 p.m. till 11 p.m. and all day on Saturday.

Walk No. 40

From the A351 Wareham to Swanage Road pass through the village of Corfe then take the B3069 turning left at Kingston. The road to Worth is signed a short distance away.

Approx. distance of walk: 3 miles OS Map 195 SY 974/776.

Although there is some limited parking at the pub and in the road outside it is better to park in the National Trust car park on the right before entering the village (presently a trust box).

Worth Matravers is one of several Purbeck villages which remain unspoilt and uncommercialized. Mostly good underfoot but quite hilly the walk takes you down to Winspit, past abandoned quarry workings and the remains of early quarrymen's cottages then along the coast path to Seacombe Cliff returning across a river valley.

From the pub turn right towards the centre of the village, go left of the duck pond walking until you reach the footpath signposted, to Winspit. Follow the path downhill over a couple of stiles, across a field and over a stile onto a gravel path which takes you straight down to Winspit.

Nearing the shore you will observe several paths leading to caves barred with iron grids - these are in place to protect the inhabitants, colonies of Greater Horseshoe bats (creatures only found in south west England and Wales) Upon reaching the cliffs turn left and join the Dorset Coast Path signposted, Seacombe ¾.

Climb the hill and follow the path along the cliff. If you are walking in the spring and pay particular attention to the ground under your feet you will almost certainly spot the early spider orchid, an extremely rare plant found only on Purbeck limestone (it is the emblem of The Dorset Trust for Nature Conservation). Continue along the path, over a couple of stiles and, after passing the disused quarry at Seacombe bear left up the field (ignore the path to the right). After rounding the hill the path descends towards a gravel track beside a small stream. Do not cross over but bear left up the valley steadily climbing the hill. About

halfway up look for a stile set in the hedge on the left, cross over and climb the very steep hillside up to another stile at the top signposted, Worth ½. Cross the field to the wall then bear right down and up the far side of the hill making for the stile set in the wall at the top which brings you onto a narrow lane leading back to the village.

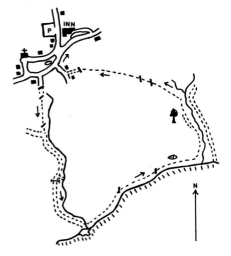

Seacombe Cliff